GRACE THAT FREES

TRADITIONS OF CHRISTIAN SPIRITUALITY SERIES

GRACE THAT FREES

The Lutheran Tradition

BRADLEY HANSON

SERIES EDITOR:
Philip Sheldrake

ORBIS BOOKS
Maryknoll, New York 10545

Founded in 1970, Orbis Books endeavors to publish works that enlighten the mind, nourish the spirit, and challenge the conscience. The publishing arm of the Maryknoll Fathers & Brothers, Orbis seeks to explore the global dimensions of the Christian faith and mission, to invite dialogue with diverse cultures and religious traditions, and to serve the cause of reconciliation and peace. The books published reflect the views of their authors and do not represent the official position of the Society. To learn more about Maryknoll and Orbis Books, please visit our website at www.maryknoll.org.

First published in Great Britian in 2004 by
Darton, Longman and Todd Ltd
1 Spencer Court
140-142 Wandsworth High Street
London SW18 4JJ

First published in the USA in 2004 by
Orbis Books
P.O. Box 308
Maryknoll, New York 10545-0308
U.S.A.

Orbis ISBN 1–57075–570–1

Printed and bound in Great Britain.

Library of Congress Cataloguing-in-Publication Data

Hanson, Bradley.
  Grace that frees : Lutheran spirituality / Bradley Hanson.
    p. cm. – (Traditions of Christian spirituality series)
  Includes bibliographical references.
  ISBN 1–57075–570–1 (pbk.)
  1. Spirituality—Lutheran Church.   2. Lutheran Church—Doctrines.
  I. Title. II. Series.
    BX8065.3.H36   2004
    248´.088´2841—dc22

                            2004007149

For Elsa,

who adds vibrancy to life.

CONTENTS

PREFACE TO THE SERIES

Nowadays, in the Western world, there is a widespread hunger for spirituality in all its forms. This is not confined to traditional religious people, let alone to regular churchgoers. The desire for resources to sustain the spiritual quest has led many people to seek wisdom in unfamiliar places. Some have turned to cultures other than their own. The fascination with Native American or Aboriginal Australian spiritualities is a case in point. Other people have been attracted by the religions of India and Tibet or the Jewish Kabbalah and Sufi mysticism. One problem is that, in comparison to other religions, Christianity is not always associated in people's minds with 'spirituality'. The exceptions are a few figures from the past who have achieved almost cult status such as Hildegard of Bingen or Meister Eckhart. This is a great pity, for Christianity East and West over two thousand years has given birth to an immense range of spiritual wisdom. Many traditions continue to be active today. Others that were forgotten are being rediscovered and reinterpreted.

It is a long time since an extended series of introductions to Christian spiritual traditions has been available in English. Given the present climate, it is an opportune moment for a new series which will help more people to be aware of the great spiritual riches available within the Christian traditions.

The overall purpose of the series is to make selected spiritual traditions available to a contemporary readership. The books seek to provide accurate and balanced historical and thematic treatments of their subjects. The authors are also conscious of the need to make connections with contemporary experience and values without being artificial or reducing a tradition to one dimension. The authors are well versed in reliable scholarship about the traditions they describe. However, their intention is that the books should be fresh in style and accessible to the general reader.

One problem that such a series inevitably faces is the word 'spirituality'. For example, it is increasingly used beyond religious circles and does not necessarily imply a faith tradition. Again, it could mean substantially different things for a Christian and a Buddhist. Within Christianity itself, the word in its modern sense is relatively recent. The reality that it stands for differs subtly in the different contexts of time and place. Historically, 'spirituality' covers a breadth of human experience and a wide range of values and practices.

No single definition of 'spirituality' has been imposed on the authors in this series. Yet, despite the breadth of the series there is a sense of a common core in the writers themselves and in the traditions they describe. All Christian spiritual traditions have their source in three things. First, while drawing on ordinary experience and even religious insights from elsewhere, Christian spiritualities are rooted in the Scriptures and particularly in the Gospels. Second, spiritual traditions are not derived from abstract theory but from attempts to live out gospel values in a positive yet critical way within specific historical and cultural contexts. Third, the experiences and insights of individuals and groups are not isolated but are related to the wider Christian tradition of beliefs, practices and community life. From a Christian perspective, spirituality is not just concerned with prayer or even with narrowly religious activities. It concerns the whole of human life, viewed in terms of a conscious relationship with God, in Jesus Christ, through the indwelling of the Holy Spirit and within a community of believers.

The series as a whole includes traditions that probably would not have appeared twenty years ago. The authors themselves have been encouraged to challenge, where appropriate, inaccurate assumptions about their particular tradition. While conscious of their own biases, authors have none the less sought to correct the imbalances of the past. Previous understandings of what is mainstream or 'orthodox' sometimes need to be questioned. People or practices that became marginal demand to be re-examined. Studies of spirituality in the past frequently underestimated or ignored the role of women. Sometimes the treatments of spiritual traditions were culturally one-sided because they were written from an uncritical Western European or North Atlantic perspective.

However, any series is necessarily selective. It cannot hope to do full justice to the extraordinary variety of Christian spiritual traditions. The principles of selection are inevitably open to question. I hope that an appropriate balance has been maintained between a sense of the likely readership on the one hand and the dangers of narrowness on the other. In the end, choices had to be made and the result is inevitably weighted in favour of traditions that have achieved 'classic' status or which seem to capture the contemporary imagination. Within these limits, I trust that the series will offer a reasonably balanced account of what the Christian spiritual tradition has to offer.

As editor of the series I would like to thank all the authors who agreed to contribute and for the stimulating conversations and correspondence that sometimes resulted. I am especially grateful for the high quality of their work which made my task so much easier. Editing such a series is a complex undertaking I have worked closely throughout with the editorial team of Darton, Longman and Todd and Robert Ellsberg of Orbis Books. I am immensely grateful to them for their friendly support and judicious advice. Without them this series would never have come together.

PHILIP SHELDRAKE
University of Durham

ACKNOWLEDGEMENTS

I wish to thank both Philip Sheldrake, editor of the Traditions of Christian Spirituality Series, for inviting me to undertake this task and Brendan Walsh, Editorial Director at Darton, Longman and Todd, for his gracious co-operation in completing the work. I am also grateful to the numerous Lutheran communities and groups with whom I have practised and discussed various aspects of Lutheran spirituality over the last four years. As always, my deepest thanks go to Marion, my wife and dearest friend, who helps make my writing possible and enjoyable.

Some explanation of certain citations is in order. *Luther's Works* will be cited as LW, volume and page; those works also in *Martin Luther's Basic Theological Writings*, edited by Timothy F. Lull, will be cited simply as Lull and page. *BC* refers to *The Book of Concord*, edited by Robert Kolb and Timothy J. Wengert (Minneapolis: Fortress, 2000); in addition to the document and article (unless given in the text), these citations will give section number rather than page number. This system works with different editions. Citations of the *Formula of Concord* will indicate which of the two main parts of that document, E for Epitome or SD for Solid Declaration. Citations from Peter Erb's 1979 selections from Johann Arndt's *True Christianity* will give book, chapter, and page. Citations from Charles Schaeffer's 1910 complete edition of books 1–4 will give book, chapter, and section.

INTRODUCTION

It has been common to regard Lutheranism from a theological point of view. Martin Luther is widely regarded as one of the very greatest of Christian theologians, one whose thought continues to reward study and inform contemporary thought. As the title of their widely used study *Lutheranism: The Theological Movement and Its Confessional Writings* indicates, two prominent Lutheran scholars, Eric Gritsch and Robert Jenson, view Lutheranism primarily as a theological movement. The importance of theology for Lutheranism is certainly not to be diminished, but it needs to be supplemented by seeing it also as a movement in spirituality. That is what this study aims to do.

The need for studying Lutheranism as a spirituality movement is especially great, because Lutheranism is sometimes regarded by both those outside and inside the tradition to be seriously deficient as spirituality, even opposed to it. When spirituality is understood as the pursuit of perfection or the intentional cultivation of holiness through certain spiritual practices, then the Lutheran emphasis on justification by grace through faith alone is often seen as contrary to it. For instance, in his pioneering history of Christian spirituality Pierre Pourrat defined spirituality as 'that part of theology which deals with Christian perfection and the ways that lead to it', and he brought Lutheranism into the discussion only with the early seventeenth-century work of Johann Arndt. While more recent scholarly surveys generally treat Luther and Lutheranism, two related attitudes are common among contemporary Lutherans. One attitude is that 'Lutheran spirituality' is an oxymoron, so those Lutherans seeking growth in this area have to go to Orthodox, Roman Catholic, or perhaps Anglican sources for help. A more negative view is that attention to spirituality is downright dangerous for Lutherans.

Much depends on the definition of spirituality. If spirituality is understood as the pursuit of holiness or sanctification, then it will be a secondary and perhaps even risky enterprise for Lutherans. But there is good reason to understand spirituality in broader terms. I suggest that there are three basic elements in a spirituality. We can identify the first two elements this way: **a spirituality is a faith with a path**.

1. *Every spirituality involves a faith which includes commitment, belief, and trust.*

a. *Commitment.* Of course, every person has many commitments – to meet a friend for lunch, to care for a family member who is ill, to complete a work assignment, and so forth. A person's faith, however, has to do with one's most fundamental commitment, that commitment which takes priority over every other. The way we can identify our actual, functioning faith is to identify what we care about most of all. What is it that matters most to us? Whatever that is, it is the object of our real faith. It may be oneself or family or power or God. Whatever we love most of all, that is the object of our faith. This ultimate commitment is a major element of faith.

b. Another element of faith is *belief.* Any faith includes a set of beliefs that makes up a picture of the world. That is, a belief says something is true, this is the way things are. We human beings tend to act in accordance with how we understand our situation. So in matters of faith, commitment and belief correspond. For example, people will give their life to God only if they believe there is a God and this God is good. Indeed, one's total picture of God powerfully influences the character of any theistic spirituality. Similarly those who have money as their highest priority in life believe that money truly is what makes the world go around. Because belief is an intrinsic factor in a spirituality, there are specific cognitive or doctrinal ingredients that distinguish one spirituality from another. So theology is a very important aspect of any Christian spirituality.

c. Faith also involves *trust*. This is the most subtle element of faith. In part, it's because we all trust in many things. We trust the steering mechanism of our car to turn the vehicle in the desired direction. We ordinarily trust our eyes and ears to give us reliable information. We have a certain trust in our closest friend. Life is not possible without trust in many things. While we sometimes speak of such instances of trust as acts of faith, the faith of which we speak here refers only to our most fundamental trust. So while we trust in many things, spirituality has to do with our ultimate trust. This may be difficult to identify, because it often becomes apparent to us only when our existence is seriously threatened. When serious illness, failure, or human betrayal strikes, then some things on which we have relied don't hold up. When ordinary securities fail, what do we depend upon? Our primary object of trust may then become evident. From a theistic perspective only God is worthy of our ultimate trust, yet in reality people are perennially tempted to place their primary trust in something else.

Commitment is the active aspect of faith in which we pour forth our caring and action. Trust is the more passive and receptive aspect of faith in which we count upon the object of our faith to support us and bring us good. Both take place within an interpretation of reality (belief) that renders this commitment and trust sensible.

2. *A spirituality also involves a path.* A path is a set of practices intended to express and nurture persons in a specific faith. Praying the Jesus Prayer day after day might be such a practice for a Christian community. To pray this prayer expresses the faith of this community, for it invokes the name of Jesus. Muslims and Jews use other repetitive prayers, while Christians use the Jesus Prayer. But praying the Jesus Prayer as a regular practice is intended to nurture members of this community in a deeper faith. When this practice is done in conjunction with other practices such as participation in

Christian liturgy, sacraments, meditation on Scripture and icons, there is a spiritual path.

An integral spirituality requires coherence of faith and practice. When I say a spirituality is a faith with a path, this does not mean that any path or practice can be combined with any faith, as though one could walk through a spirituality buffet and mix and match items at will. Coherence requires integration of faith and practice. One might borrow a particular practice from a different spiritual tradition, even a different religion. Yet if it is not to be merely a discordant patch stuck on a garment, the practice must be reinterpreted and integrated into one's faith.

This coherence of faith and practice becomes obvious in the origins of Lutheran spirituality. Martin Luther objected to a practice of indulgences, because he believed the biblical notion of repentance involved more. But Luther had not yet arrived at his pivotal insight of justification by grace through faith alone. When he did come to his pivotal insight some months later, he rather quickly called for much more extensive changes in Christian spiritual practices. Faith and path go together.

3. *The faith and path of a spirituality are lived out in a certain social, historical context.* Because we human beings live within the concrete realities of a specific social and historical context, we never approach the issues of faith and spiritual practice as an isolated individual with a blank slate. We always navigate in some sort of social boat on a temporal river flowing with various cultural and religious currents.

We must also take the social, historical context into account when trying to understand Lutheran spirituality. While Lutheranism began in some sense with Martin Luther, he certainly thought of his mission as calling the Church away from aberrations in faith and practice back to its roots in biblical spirituality. So Lutheran spirituality is significantly shaped by its origins as a sixteenth-century reform movement in western Christianity. Yet Lutheran spirituality is not simply to be equated with the spirituality of Martin Luther, for the Lutheran movement continued to develop as its adherents encountered new circumstances and different cultural contexts. Today there are Lutherans in diverse cultures on many continents. What lends considerable coherence to Lutheran spirituality, though, is dialogue with its foundations in Martin Luther and the Lutheran confessional writings.

I have chosen to entitle this study on Lutheran spirituality *Grace That Frees*. While there is no question that grace has been a central concern and enduring theme among Lutherans, one might wonder whether freedom has been so prominent. Yet the content and spirit of Martin Luther's faith and theology is no better articulated than in his 1520 treatise *The Freedom of a Christian*, and he chose to name a second major treatise of that year *The Babylonian Captivity of the Church*. In addition, his own theological writing in which he took considerable pride was *The Bondage of the Will*. Clearly questions of freedom and bondage both in faith and religious practice were very important in Luther's thought, and they are sounded frequently in the sixteenth-century Lutheran confessional writings. Grace and freedom figure prominently both in Lutheran theology and spirituality.

Our discussion will pay special attention to these themes as we consider the faith, path, and historical development of Lutheran spirituality. Chapter one will give an historical overview of Lutheranism; chapters two to four treat three major aspects of Lutheran faith; and chapters five to eight deal with major practices in the Lutheran path.

1. FAITH, PRACTICE, AND HISTORY

In spirituality there is mutual interaction between faith and path, faith and practice. The ancient formula for this is *lex orandi, lex credendi*. Grammatically this formula can mean either the rule of prayer is a norm for belief or the reverse, the rule of belief is a norm for prayer. This linguistic ambiguity reflects the interaction in history between worship and doctrine, which in turn is part of the broad interplay of faith and practice in spirituality. The predominant Roman Catholic interpretation of *lex orandi, lex credendi* has been that worship practice is an authority for doctrine. None the less, there have been instances in which the magisterium also deliberately introduced certain worship practices, in order to promote a particular doctrine. An example, cited by Pope Pius IX, is the introduction of the Feast of the Immaculate Conception by some of his predecessors to help prepare the way for his proclamation of that dogma in 1854. In the background, of course, is the conviction that the Holy Spirit's guidance of the Church is such that neither the Church's worship nor the teaching of the hierarchy over time will depart from Christian truth in any important way. Hence, both historic worship and authoritative teaching of the magisterium are considered reliable.[1]

The predominant approach among Lutherans has been to emphasize the rule of faith as the norm for worship and religious practice generally, yet there are also instances in which practice has been an authority for belief. Luther's handling of the liturgy exemplifies the approach to spiritual practices taken generally by him and articulated in the Lutheran

Confessions. Unlike some Protestants who sought to return to worship patterns of the New Testament Church, Lutherans did not repudiate the Roman or western rite liturgy that had developed over the centuries. Nevertheless, worship forms should be consistent with Scripture and the central doctrine of grace, justification by grace through faith in Jesus Christ. So Lutherans offered both bread and wine to the laity in Holy Communion as agreeable with Scripture. Another major change Luther made in his Latin liturgy and German liturgy was to excise language of sacrifice, which he believed suggested that humans are offering something to God in addition to Christ's sacrifice on the cross. Thus, the witness of Scripture and its core teachings are invoked as the norm for worship and devotional practices. Yet at times Lutherans have used liturgy to illustrate and protect sound doctrine.[2]

In order to understand Lutheran spirituality in its various forms over time, we will trace some major events and movements in Lutheran history. This begins with the reform movement led by Martin Luther.

The Lutheran Reformation

About 4.00 p.m. on 17 April 1521 Martin Luther was shown into a meeting of Emperor Charles V and German political leaders in the bishop's residence in Worms, Germany. This Diet of Worms had been conducting various secular affairs since January, but now it needed also to attend to the religious controversy centred on Luther that had been brewing for over three years. As he entered, Luther recognized a friend and spoke to him, but was instructed by his imperial escort not to speak without being asked. Johann von der Eck, Chancellor of the Archbishop of Trier, addressed Luther first in Latin and then in German. He said the emperor had summoned Luther for two reasons – to see whether he would acknowledge as his own the books printed under his name and whether he wished to affirm or retract anything in them. A pile of Luther's books was on a table. Before he could answer, a lawyer for Luther's prince, Frederick the Wise of Electoral Saxony, asked that the titles of the books be read out. They were.

Luther answered first in German and then in Latin. One observer wrote, 'He spoke with a subdued, soft voice, as if frightened and shocked, with little calm in his visage and gestures, also with little deference in his attitude and countenance.'[3] Responding to the first question, Luther said that the books were his. In regard to the second question whether he would affirm or deny their contents, he said this was a very serious matter and it would be wrong to speak in haste. In order to avoid harm to either God's Word or his own salvation, he humbly requested additional time to consider his answer. Luther was most likely surprised by the second question. He had hoped for a discussion of disputed issues, rather than a mere demand to confirm or recant his teachings. In turn his request for more time surprised the assembly, but after some consultation and a warning from von der Eck that Luther should renounce his errors or face serious penalties, he was granted one more day.

Luther realized the threat to his safety. Some of his views were already linked with those of John Hus, who had been burned at the stake for heresy in 1415 during the Council of Constance, even though he had been given an imperial safe conduct. The mightiest powers of Luther's day – pope and emperor – were against him. Pope Leo X had excommunicated him some months earlier and threatened those who protected him with excommunication and interdict. Less than a month previously the emperor had condemned Luther's books and ordered them to be taken out of circulation; the remaining question for Charles was what to do with the person of Luther. The chief powers protecting Luther were his own prince, Frederick the Wise, and widespread public support in Germany. So his situation was extremely precarious.

The same time next day Luther was again escorted to the bishop's residence, but the press of business forced him to wait in a crowd until six o'clock. The members of the Diet were in a larger, crowded room that now was lit with torches and hot.

Luther stood in the midst of the princes. Von der Eck again stated the two questions and admonished him to answer. In German and then Latin Luther spoke humbly but in a loud voice without fear. On the question of whether he would defend or retract anything in his books, Luther divided them into three groups. Some treated faith so soundly that even his opponents had to admit they were useful. Other books criticized those who were undermining Christian faith, and many agreed with his criticisms. To recant these books would only add to the tyranny and evil. A third group of books was against individuals who defended the Roman tyranny and attacked his suggested reforms; these writings he could not retract unless refuted from Scripture. In the hot room Luther was sweating profusely.

Von der Eck replied that Luther should not arrogantly think he alone understood Scripture, and then demanded that he answer without qualification whether he would recant his books. To this Luther responded, 'Unless I am convinced by the testimony of the Scriptures or by clear reason (for I do not trust either in the pope or in councils alone, since it is well known that they have often erred and contradicted themselves), I am bound by the Scriptures I have quoted and my conscience is captive to the Word of God. I cannot and I will not retract anything, since it is neither safe nor right to go against conscience. May God help me. Amen.'[4]

As two imperial aides escorted Luther out, people asked whether he was being taken prisoner. The aides said no, but moments later another imperial attendant yelled, 'To the pyre with him!' Next morning, 19 April, the emperor had read to the leaders his own written view of the matter in which he stated his clear opposition to Luther, but they wanted to make one more attempt at resolving the dispute through negotiation. On 22 April the emperor granted three more days to obtain Luther's recantation; then his ban would be imposed. The German leaders formed a commission of ten members to negotiate, and discussions took place on 24 and 25 April without a change in Luther's stance. On the evening of the 25th Luther was informed that the emperor would take action against him, but he had twenty-one days to return home before his safe conduct would expire. The emperor then issued the Edict of Worms that declared Luther an 'obstinate schismatic and manifest heretic' who was to be taken prisoner and delivered to the emperor.[5]

How did Martin Luther come to such an extraordinary situation? The outward course of his earlier life was not exceptional for his time. In 1505, not quite at the age of twenty-two, he had entered the monastery of Augustinian Hermits in Erfurt. The monks in this order were no longer hermits, for in 1256 the pope had called them to give spiritual care in the cities. Luther never said why he chose this order or monastery among the many available, but it belonged to an association of reformed Augustinian monasteries under vicar Johann von Staupitz. These reformed communities strictly observed the monastic rule of Augustine. Luther was ordained a priest in 1507, and was selected to study theology. He must have earned the trust and respect of Staupitz, because in late 1510 he and another monk were sent to negotiate some organizational issues with the head of the order in Rome. He both studied and taught philosophy and theology until he received his doctor of theology degree in 1512. Earlier that same year Luther was transferred from Erfurt to the Augustinian monastery in Wittenberg where he became subprior and preacher for the monks and professor of Bible at the fledgling university established in the capital of Electoral Saxony. As far as we know, he started lecturing on the Bible with the 1513–14 semester.[6] In 1515 he was elected district vicar over ten monasteries.[7]

While the outward course of Luther's early life was not extraordinary, inwardly he struggled for a number of years. Scholars are not entirely sure about the nature and timing of this struggle and its resolution, but it appears the crux was how he could be in proper relationship with God. The theology and piety he learned led him to understand God as a strict judge, and Christ was no help since he too was a judge. Genuine repentance was a critical issue for him personally.

Most likely Luther had not resolved his own theological and spiritual questions when an indulgence campaign began in nearby towns in 1517. Indulgences were a common spiritual practice of the time associated with penance. According to accepted teaching, God forgave guilt and freed the penitent sinner from eternal punishment, but the sinner was still liable to temporal punishment. Any temporal punishment still due after death was removed in purgatory. Strictly defined, an indulgence reduced or removed only temporal punishment. However, the careful distinction between guilt of sin and temporal punishment was blurred by the indulgence preacher John Tetzel. His instructions claimed complete forgiveness of all sins for the recipient and of all temporal punishment for the recipient or a dead person in purgatory. Conditions for receiving this grace were contrition, confession, offering prayers in seven churches, and payment according to one's status. The campaign attracted some people from Wittenberg who then sought absolution from Luther the priest. He believed there was more to repentance.

After some months of preaching against the indulgence, on 31 October Luther wrote a humble letter of protest to Archbishop Albrecht and his diocesan Bishop of Brandenburg, and also issued ninety-five theses for academic debate. Luther did not yet know that Albrecht had made an agreement with the papacy in which half the indulgence revenue would go to the papacy for building St Peter's Basilica in Rome and the other half to Albrecht to cover his fees to the papacy for obtaining the archbishopric. In any case, Luther wanted to address indulgences and repentance on both the practical and theoretical levels. Within a few weeks, however, others translated his Latin theses into German, printed and distributed them widely, and a controversy erupted.[8]

Luther's pastoral concern for ordinary people prompted him to criticize the indulgence, but many scholars today do not think he had yet come to his new understanding of grace. In 1545 Luther said this new insight came afterward while pondering Romans 1:17, 'For in it the righteousness of God is revealed through faith for faith; as it is written, "The one who is righteous will live by faith."' He hated the 'righteousness of God', for he had been taught to understand it as that quality by which God punishes the unrighteous sinner. But attention to the context led him to see it as the righteousness by which God mercifully justifies the person of faith.[9] This is the nucleus of Luther's central conviction of justification by grace through faith. Some scholars have questioned the accuracy of his memory which seems to place this insight in 1518 some months after the indulgence controversy began, but many others accept it.[10] In any case, all scholars see in Luther's early writings a gradual shift in his thinking over several years.

After the controversy began, Luther's thinking also developed on another critical issue – authority. In a meeting with papal legate Cardinal Cajetan in October 1518, Luther denied that the pope had the authority to authorize indulgences. At a ten-day debate with theologian John Eck in the summer of 1519, in Leipzig, Luther went further: councils as well as popes could err; Scripture is the highest authority. Luther's reliance on the primary authority of Scripture is evident in his stance at Worms.

As Luther's central conviction about justification revamped his understanding of the proper relationship with God, he extended his call for reform of spiritual practice and church life into other areas with three major treatises in the latter half of 1520. Major proposed changes were reception of both Eucharistic bread and wine by laity, rejection of the Eucharist as a sacrifice offered to God, and an end of private masses on which monasteries and clergy relied heavily for their income. So, when Luther appeared before the Diet of Worms in April 1521, he had not only challenged indulgences, but many features of late medieval theology and spirituality.

Following the Diet of Worms the evangelical reform movement spread within Germany and beyond. Luther's ideas struck a responsive chord with many among the broad range of those who felt a need for reformation in the Church. Although a sizeable group wanted merely moral and administrative amendment and others sought more radical changes in theology and practice than Luther, many largely agreed with his call for reform centred in justification by faith. Even though the emperor's edict had declared Luther an outlaw who could be killed without reprisal, his prince had him whisked away to Wartburg Castle where he remained incognito for ten months.

But when major changes in worship, some of which Luther personally approved, were hastily imposed in Wittenberg by university colleague Carlstadt, Luther returned and restored order by preaching that love does not force people in matters of faith. Following Paul's 1 Corinthians 8 distinction between the strong and weak of faith, Luther urged that gospel freedom called for patience and sound preaching, not compulsion.[11] Reform of churches in cities or territories with sympathetic leaders went forward; evangelical pastors were installed and new church orders were instituted. When church visitations in 1528 revealed widespread religious ignorance among the common people, the following year Luther published his *Small Catechism* and *Large Catechism*.

Efforts to restore church unity continued, inspired in part by political concerns. In 1530, at a Diet called in Augsburg by Emperor Charles V, the Lutherans were to present a statement of faith and major points of difference on practical matters. Since he was still under ban, Luther stayed several days' ride away. His close associate Philip Melanchthon wrote the *Augsburg Confession*, which briefly stated the chief articles of their faith and then described their views on some disputed practical matters. In its conclusion Melanchthon claimed that 'nothing has been accepted among us, in teaching or ceremonies, that is contrary to Scripture or the catholic church.'[12] Luther heartily approved of the document, although he chafed at Melanchthon's side-efforts to negotiate an agreement making minimal concessions to Lutheran practice. John Eck wrote the *Catholic Confutation of the Augsburg Confession*, and the emperor demanded that all the political leaders sign it. Several weeks later Melanchthon responded with his detailed defence, the *Apology of the Augsburg Confession*, but the emperor declined to receive it. When Melanchthon left Augsburg the situation looked so dark for the reform cause that several reform-minded princes created a military alliance, the Schmalcald League. This alliance and the emperor's need for their financial assistance against the Turks seeking to advance further into Europe led to an agreement that gave the Protestants religious freedom until a free church council would meet.

After the Diet of Augsburg European society was religiously divided into Roman Catholic, Lutheran, Reformed (led by Zwingli and later Calvin in Switzerland), various radical reformation groups (commonly distinguished as Anabaptists, Spiritualists, and Evangelical Rationalists), and soon the Church of England.[13] Sporadic attempts at reunion continued. In 1537 preparing for a church council that never happened, Luther wrote a statement of faith called the *Smalcald Articles* and Melanchthon the *Treatise on the Power and Primacy of the Pope*. The reform movement led by Luther settled into a number of distinct territorial churches mostly in northern Europe. Catholic military defeat of Lutheran princes in 1547 threatened to snuff out the Lutheran reform movement, but military reversal several years later brought about the 1555 Peace of Augsburg that gave each prince the power to determine the religion of his territory, whether Catholic, Lutheran, or Reformed. This ended major wars over religion in Germany until the Thirty Years' War began in 1618. So political stability of Lutheran territories was achieved.

Doctrinal consolidation also took place. Many social movements start with a founder's fresh initiatives and then enter a phase in which the next generation tries to preserve the founding vision. This was true also of Lutheranism. After Luther died in 1546, there were several theological disputes among Lutherans. These were largely settled with careful treatment of the issues in the *Formula of Concord* (1577). The *Book of Concord* (1580) brought together all the Lutheran confessional documents: the ancient Apostles', Nicene, and Athanasian

Creeds, *Augsburg Confession*, *Apology of the Augsburg Confession*, *Smalcald Articles*, *Treatise on the Power and Primacy of the Pope*, *Small Catechism*, *Large Catechism*, and *Formula of Concord*. The Church in Denmark and Norway took as its standard the *Augsburg Confession* and *Small Catechism*, while the Church in Sweden and Finland later accepted the whole *Book of Concord* while giving primacy to the *Augsburg Confession*.

Later Movements

After 1580 Lutheran church life and theology were dominated for a century by a concern that was dear to Luther himself, correct doctrine; this stance is called Lutheran Orthodoxy. A number of theologians composed massive scholarly volumes. An early representative was Martin Chemnitz (1522–86), who was a key figure in writing the *Formula of Concord* and produced the premier Lutheran response to the Council of Trent, whose intermittent sessions between 1945 and 1963 reasserted Catholic doctrine and spiritual practices. Johann Gerhard (1582–1637), the greatest Lutheran Orthodox theologian, used Aristotle's philosophy, although it had been rejected by Luther. A later representative was Johann Quenstedt (1617–88). The Lutheran Orthodox theologians rigorously defended Lutheran teaching over against other views, especially Roman Catholic and Reformed. The background for many of these polemics was political strife along religious lines and even the horrendously costly Thirty Years' War (1618–48). In stressing biblical authority over against Catholic teaching, the Orthodox theologians generally asserted inerrancy of the Bible.

Some conditions were not conducive to spiritual life during this period. Lutheran Orthodox theologians focused pastoral education on pure doctrine and polemics against other theological views, so many pastors delivered learned sermons unconnected with ordinary life. In addition, territorial princes, who controlled major ecclesiastical appointments, were often more interested in the Church's contribution to civil order than in spiritual life; some imposed fines for those not attending church. So spirituality under Lutheran Orthodox leadership was burdened with considerable head religion and outward conformity.

Nevertheless, there were also signs of deep spiritual life during the period of Orthodoxy. One sign was the composition of much fine hymnody and religious music. While Philip Nicolai (1556–1608) was interested in theological polemics and writing a devotional work, he also wrote many hymns such as the words and music for 'Wake, Awake, for Night is Flying' (Wachet Auf). Other important hymn writers were: Johann Heermann (1585–1647), 'Ah, Holy Jesus'; Martin Rinkert (1586–1649), 'Now Thank We All Our God'; Johann Franck (1618–77), 'Jesus, Priceless Treasure'; Paul Gerhardt (1606-76), 'A Lamb Goes Uncomplaining Forth' and a free rendering of Bernard of Clairvaux's 'O Sacred Head Now Wounded'; and in Denmark Thomas Kingo (1634–1703), 'On My Heart Imprint Your Image'. In addition, many excellent motets and cantatas were composed by Michael Praetorius (1571–1621), Heinrich Schutz (1585–1672), and J.S. Bach (1685–1750).[14]

Another sign of spiritual life during the age of Orthodoxy was the publication of some widely read devotional works. Beside producing great theology books, Johann Gerhard wrote two popular devotional works. He published *Sacred Meditations* in 1606 when he was only twenty-four years old. Other significant devotional writings were Heinrich Muller's *Spiritual Hours of Refreshment* (1664) and Christian Scriver's *Gotthold's Occasional Devotions* (1663–9).[15]

The most influential devotional work, though, was by Johann Arndt (1555–1621), a pastor who expressed many of the concerns later picked up by Pietists. Arndt called for a reduction in polemics and a focus on genuine repentance. He thought many were taking God's grace for granted, so he stressed a Christ-centred faith that issued in a holy life. His *True Christianity*, first published in 1605 and enlarged in 1610, became the most influential devotional work ever in

Lutheranism. Lutherans emigrating to America commonly took with them a Bible, hymn-book, and *True Christianity*. Although Arndt drew criticism from some defenders of orthodoxy for his use of mystical writings that compromised the doctrine of justification, he was supported by Johann Gerhard and others.

Arndt's concerns were later given organizational life in the Pietist movement led by Philip Jacob Spener (1635–1705), a pastor working in Frankfurt am Main. In 1675 Spener made some proposals in a preface to a new edition of Arndt's sermons. Spener's preface was soon issued under its own title, *Pia Desideria* (Pious Desires). His six recommendations provided a definite programme for change for the Arndtian reform tradition. They were:

(1) More extensive use of the Word of God. In addition to reading more of Scripture in worship and the home, he advocated small gatherings for reflection on the Bible. Spener had started these conventicles or *collegia pietatis* five years before, and they became one of the distinguishing marks of the Pietist movement.

(2) Emphasis on the priesthood of all believers. This increased the responsibility of laity for the spiritual nurture of others and reduced their social distance from clergy.

(3) The importance of love over theological knowledge. To help put this into practice, Spener suggested entering into a confidential relationship with one's confessor or spiritual guide.

(4) Greater kindness in religious controversies. One reason Spener gave is that hope for unity among Christian confessional groups cannot be based on argumentation alone.

(5) Greater attention to holiness of life in the education and selection of pastors, since it is they who bear the greatest responsibility for reform of the Church. He recommended that the theological faculty participate with students in a conventicle.

(6)   More practical education for pastors, in that the true purpose of sermons, sacraments, and catechism is 'faith and its fruits'.[16]

Leadership of the movement in the next generation passed to August Hermann Francke (1663–1727) who made the University of Halle the main training ground for Pietist pastors. Unlike his predecessor, Francke taught that a conversion experience was God's usual way of working. While Spener concentrated on renewal of the Church, Francke created new charitable and mission institutions for the renewal of society as well as the Church. However, legalistic strains also came to the fore with Francke.

Although the contrast between Orthodoxy and Pietism should not be overplayed, on the whole Lutheran Orthodoxy emphasized the head and Pietism the heart. So while Orthodoxy produced many books of academic theology, Lutheran Pietism produced very few of note. Pietist small group meetings encouraged personal sharing and free prayer. In public worship, the Orthodox stressed appreciation of the riches embedded in the historic orders, whereas Pietists sought forms that would touch the heart.[17]

The great scientific achievements of the seventeenth century and especially Isaac Newton's contributions ushered in an age of Enlightenment in much of European culture. While some intellectuals attacked religion, most sought to prove that religion was compatible with science. Isaac Newton was a devout man who spoke of two books by which God is known – the Bible and nature. The common result was to stress belief in God the creator and morality and to minimize sin and Jesus Christ as Saviour. Where rationalist thinking was strong, participation in worship and Holy Communion dropped substantially, and Holy Communion was often detached from the main service. This outlook was especially dominant in Christian Wolff (1679–1754) and later in the great German philosopher Immanuel Kant (1724–1804). Rationalism was strong in Germany, Denmark, and among Lutherans in America where

John Locke's philosophy shaped the thinking of many, but less in Sweden and still less in Norway and Finland.

The currents of Orthodoxy, Pietism, and rationalism did not supplant and succeed one another, but rather often co-existed within Lutheranism. Rationalism continued among some intellectuals. But new life was breathed into Orthodox concerns with the Neo-Lutheran movement that renewed attention to Luther and the Lutheran Confessions in connection with the 300-year anniversary of the Ninety-five Theses in 1817 and the Prussian king's decree to unify the Lutheran and Reformed Churches. One Neo-Lutheran leader was Wilhelm Loehe (1808–72) who combined the confessional emphasis with high church worship and frequent Eucharist. Rationalism was also countered during the late seventeenth and early eighteenth centuries by Pietist revivals in Sweden, Norway, Finland, and Denmark. In the United States, too, by the 1840s the strong rationalist influence of the colonial period had waned, but some Lutherans (e.g. Missouri Synod) were predominantly Orthodox and others (e.g. Eilsen Synod) predominantly Pietist. Yet Orthodox and Pietist strains often intermingled within the same synod. These two orientations continue within Lutheranism today, although they may no longer carry the labels of Orthodoxy and Pietism. Rather, Orthodox concerns are maintained by those who stress adherence to the Lutheran Confessions and historic liturgical forms, while Pietist concerns are carried by those who emphasize personal faith experiences, reaching the unchurched, and using contemporary revivalist worship forms.

In addition to large emigrations from Europe to North America, Lutherans have taken root on every continent. Significant numbers of Germans emigrated to Brazil, Australia, and Southern Africa in the nineteenth century. In addition, mission societies, often with government support, sent Pietist missionaries to German, Danish, and Swedish colonies, as well as other lands. For instance, the Danish government in collaboration with Halle Pietists sent a missionary to its colony in Tranquebar, India in 1706. German missionaries started work in Tanzania in 1890, and were joined by Scandinavian and North American missionaries when it became a British colony after the First World War. Fuelled by energetic evangelism and a high birth rate, the Evangelical Lutheran Church of Tanzania currently is growing rapidly. Today third-world Lutherans are about one out of every six Lutherans. Yet while the sixty-million Lutherans worldwide are heavily European in ethnic background, growth is largely among other ethnic peoples.[18]

Meanwhile, Lutheran churches in Europe and North America have declined in membership and participation as they have faced terrible wars, secularism, and postmodern cynicism about belief systems and social institutions. In Europe throughout the twentieth century until today more and more people have become alienated from the Church. For instance in Sweden, although many contemporary young people get confirmed in the Lutheran Church as a socially accepted rite of passage, very few attend worship. Sweden is now one of the most secularized nations in the world. In the United States Lutheran churches grew through immigration and strong birth rate until about 1970, but since then either slightly negative or barely positive annual growth has kept them behind population growth.

Ecumenism

The issue of unity among Christians has been dealt with variously by Lutherans down through their history. Luther, Melanchthon, and their supporters set out to reform the western Roman Catholic Church, not found a separate Church; in spite of repeated attempts on all sides for agreement, though, that was the result. What followed was theological trench warfare by many. The Orthodox asserted the Lutheran Church to be the true Church over against other Christian communities, most of whom made the same claim. Pietists, concerned more for renewed lives than for doctrine, tended to be ecumenical for their time. Spener read the writings of Puritan and Reformed leaders and had personal contact with them. Francke even had hope for reunion with Roman Catholics. However, it was nineteenth-century involvement in mission efforts that promoted co-operation across denominational lines and gave birth to the ecumenical movement.

Lutheran ecumenical efforts have taken place chiefly on two fronts – with other Lutheran churches and with other denominations. While one national Church was the rule in the Scandinavian countries, there were multiple Lutheran bodies in Germany, North America, and in many other countries. Government pressure inspired representatives of the German territorial Churches to come together in 1868 at a General Evangelical Lutheran Conference. Churches in several other countries sent representatives to later Conference meetings. In the United States Lutherans first organized along ethnic lines, but geography and theology also were factors. At one point in the late nineteenth century there were sixty-six distinct Lutheran churches, although most also participated in one of three Lutheran associations. Global Lutheran ties reached a new level with the first Lutheran World Convention in 1923. It changed its name in 1947 to the Lutheran World Federation and most Lutheran churches now belong to it. Largest of those that do not belong is the US body Lutheran Church–Missouri Synod, which insists on a higher degree of doctrinal unity.

Lutheran churches and leaders have participated in the broader ecumenical movement since the first World Missionary Conference in 1910. Swedish archbishop Nathan Soederdblom (1866–1931) initiated the ecumenical Life and Work movement and presided over its first World Conference in Stockholm in 1925. However, with their strong interest in sound doctrine, Lutherans tended to be cautious about rushing things. After the formation of the World Council of Churches in 1948, they became more involved and today most Lutheran churches belong. None the less, still today some such as the Lutheran Church–Missouri Synod do not participate. In addition, beginning with the Church of England and Scandinavian Churches dialogue in 1908, Lutherans have participated in many bilateral dialogues. Perhaps the most significant of these have been national and international dialogues with Roman Catholic representatives after the Second Vatican Council. A major step was taken with the signing of the *Joint Declaration on the Doctrine of Justification* on 31 October 1999 in Augsburg, Germany by representatives of the Lutheran World Federation and the Vatican.

With this historical survey as background, now we will turn directly to the discussion of Lutheran spirituality. We will focus first on the Lutheran understanding of two fundamental elements in Christian faith – the human predicament and salvation. We begin with the human predicament.

2. SIN AND GOD'S PRIOR INITIATIVE

'I believe that by my own understanding or strength I cannot believe in Jesus Christ my Lord or come to him, but instead the Holy Spirit has called me through the gospel, enlightened me with his gifts, made me holy and kept me in the true faith . . .'[1] This explanation to the third article of the creed from Luther's *Small Catechism* speaks to two fundamental human questions. How serious is the human predicament? And who is able to set this predicament right?

All Christians say the basic human problem is alienation from God – sin. All Christian traditions also agree that we are unable of ourselves to set things right: God must come to our aid. However, there are significant differences over the contribution of humans to setting things right. Many Christian traditions hold that God has the primary part in healing the relationship, but they claim humans must help bring it about. The most popular version of this is that God offers the gift of salvation to a person and then it is up to that person to accept or refuse the gift. In the minds of many, such a view does justice both to God and humans. Salvation is God's gift, not something earned by human beings, yet God leaves it up to people to receive or reject the gift. It appears to concur with Luther's statement that by my own understanding or strength I cannot believe in Jesus Christ.

Yet Luther and the Lutheran Confessions express serious reservations about this popular view. Their reservations are chiefly two. One is that in this popular view human beings are portrayed as having free choice in relation to God, and the Lutheran Confessions, like Augustine, deny that we have free will in relation to God. This Lutheran claim is shocking to many, for it runs counter to a widely held assumption that free will is an innate human capacity in all matters. The other reservation stated in the Lutheran Confessions is that the popular view understands God as being more passive than is truly the case. That is, in the popular view God appears like a dedicated salesperson who makes an impassioned pitch, but then must leave the final decision in the hands of the buyer. The Lutheran view is that God is more profoundly active in bringing about the positive response of faith. The Lutheran view needs some explanation.

Part of the explanation comes with understanding the nature of faith in God. The complex reality of faith in God includes trust, belief, commitment, obedience, and hope, yet for Luther the central element is trust in or reliance on God. When trust in God is understood as central to faith, then sin is fundamentally lack of trust in God or, more strongly, distrust of God. While sin includes many specific acts of wrongdoing and hurting others, the root sin is distrust of God. In this respect, Luther agrees with Augustine that the basic sin of Adam and Eve came prior to eating of the forbidden fruit when, at the serpent's suggestion, they doubted God. Coming to faith is then the movement from distrust of God to trust, a fundamental reorientation of a person's life.

Another part of the explanation is to show that the transition from distrust of God to trust is a profound change in a person's life stance, not a simple matter of choice. We can make the point by analogy through the following story.

Imagine that Beth is a nine-year-old girl who was abandoned by her father when she was a toddler and three years later by her alcoholic mother. Next Beth lived with relatives, a while with this one, a while with that one, before the State took over her care. At various times since her earliest years Beth has been physically and sexually abused. Now at age nine you meet her and want to help her. You want to be her friend. You would like her to trust you. In fact, you even say to her, 'You can trust me.' However, Beth is a girl who doesn't trust anyone beside herself, for harsh experience has taught her repeatedly that other people are unreliable and often dangerous. So you are not surprised when she fails to respond as you ask.

The critical question for our purposes is whether at this point in her life Beth is *able* to trust you. There is good reason to say that she is not. It's not just that she *won't* trust you, for that implies that she could if she wished. Rather, right now she *cannot* trust you. The reason is that trust is not something that we simply decide to do; it is not subject to our volition. We can decide many things in life. Most of us can choose what to eat for breakfast, what shirt to wear, what sort of work to do, maybe even what person to marry. However, there are some stances of the self that are not directly controlled by our will. Trust is one. Worry or anxiety is another. If we are terribly worried about something and someone tells us, 'Don't worry', we're not able to stop worrying. Although we can strive to manage our worry so that it does not cripple us, we are unable to turn it off by choice. Similarly, trust is a stance that cannot be turned on and off at will.

How will Beth ever come to rely upon you as a friend? It might happen if you treat her kindly and stay by her through thick and thin. Mostly likely she will test you, act up to see whether you too will abandon her. Let's say that after many months or even years of steady support and acceptance on your part, she comes to trust you. How has this profound change come about? Your treatment of her has made it possible for her to trust you. Whereas previously she was strictly unable to trust anyone, your reliable behaviour has enabled her to trust you.

Of course, at some point in this development, Beth became conscious of giving her trust to you. She may even have experienced this as choosing to trust you. But her choosing to trust you comes late in the game. What preceded and made it possible is your kind treatment of her. It's also possible that Beth might persist in her distrust and never trust you. In that case she would remain in her prison of distrust.

Beth's story illustrates what Luther and the Lutheran

Confessions say about faith in God. According to them, we all place our basic trust in something; no one is neutral. Since we are born into a world ruled by idolatry, we learn to have confidence in a creature and mistrust God. This most basic orientation of the self cannot be turned around by our choice. To be sure, we are free to manage our lives in many ways. Circumstances allowing, we can choose what to eat and what to wear, we can choose a job and marriage partner. These choices belong to what the Lutheran Confessions call freedom in matters below us and civil righteousness. We may even choose to be extremely observant in our religious practice. But nothing we can do, religious or secular, can bring about that fundamental reorientation of the self that enables us to rely upon God. In fact, strict religious practice can be just another form of reliance on human resources. Rather, it is God's steadfast love and acceptance that win our confidence and evoke that new response of trusting God. God's grace sets us free from the bondage in which sin rules our life.

In some cases a person is aware of choosing God, even of making a 'decision for Christ'. Nevertheless, any experience of choosing God comes late in the process and is made possible by God's gracious action toward us. God's loving action toward us makes it possible for us to entrust our life to God. On our own we are unable to break free of our distrust. Faith is a response to God's prior action. God's grace sets people free from the bondage of idolatry and its destructive allies. So faith is entirely a gift of God's prior gracious initiative.

This teaching about sin and faith is meant as a corollary to justification by grace alone through faith alone. The pessimistic teaching about sin is intended to help ward off mistaken opinions that the reformers believed promote spiritual bondage. Luther himself had experienced a system of thought and practice that had fostered in him and many others a relationship with God that was like a transaction. If people were diligent in doing their small part, then God would handle the greater part. In much nominalist theology of the late Middle Ages this transactional relationship was encouraged by a relatively optimistic reading of the human situation which included the theological injunction 'to do what is in one's power', *facere quod in se est*. While this injunction was commonly understood to mean that God would deal generously with our feeble efforts, it also could have the effect of urging people to strive harder to become acceptable to God.[2] After all, how could one know whether one had done all that is in one's power? Connected with this reading of the human situation was an optimistic interpretation of merit. Some late medieval theology taught that a person could gain both merit for deeds done by human natural powers and merit for actions arising from divine grace.

Purchasing indulgences was only one means for achieving merit with God. A wide variety of available liturgical and devotional practices such as endowing private masses, going on pilgrimages, giving devotion to Mary, and venerating the relics of saints could also be turned to this end.[3] Luther critiqued many of the religious practices of his time. He called for the elimination of some, such as private masses and prayers to saints, but mainly he objected to what he regarded as a *false opinion* about devotional practices and other good works, namely that they were in some measure a means for becoming acceptable to God. To fall prey to this false opinion was to submit to spiritual bondage and to open oneself and others to a terrified conscience, unsure of how one stood with God. The Lutheran pessimistic interpretation of the human condition and the insistence that faith is wholly God's gift are meant to help free believers from this bondage. It does so in part by challenging the deep motivation for such religious efforts to win God's approval – the desire to remain in control vis-à-vis God.

The Roman Catholic Council of Trent in its decrees on original sin and justification in 1546 and 1547 took a somewhat less optimistic view of the human condition than most nominalist theology, so it was closer to the Lutheran Confessions. Nevertheless, some differences in emphasis remain. This agreement and difference also appear in the *Joint Declaration on the Doctrine of Justification* signed by representatives of the

Lutheran World Federation and the Roman Catholic Church in 1999. Included within its consensus on basic truths of justification is an article on human powerlessness and sin in which the agreement about free will in relation to God is substantial:

> 19. We confess together that all persons depend completely on the saving grace of God for their salvation. The freedom they possess in relation to persons and the things of this world is no freedom in relation to salvation, for as sinners they stand under God's judgment and are incapable of turning by themselves to God to seek deliverance . . .

This is a very significant agreement. Nevertheless, not all preaching and teaching in either Lutheran or Catholic churches is consistent with this formal statement. Furthermore, there are some remaining differences which are not great enough to break the basic consensus. The Declaration refers to some of these differences when it goes on to say,

> 20. When Catholics say that persons 'cooperate' in preparing for and accepting justification by consenting to God's justifying action, they see such personal consent as itself an effect of grace, not an action arising from innate human abilities.
> 21. According to Lutheran teaching, human beings are incapable of cooperating in their salvation because as sinners they actively oppose God and his saving action. Lutherans do not deny that a person can reject the working of grace.[4]

One major source of remaining difference seems to be that Roman Catholic theology interprets the sinful state of humans as a privation or lack of supernatural gifts which would enable them to relate properly to God, whereas Lutheran theology sees the sinful state as active opposition to God. So in the Catholic view there is more neutral or positive potential to be tapped for reconnecting with God, while in the Lutheran outlook there is active resistance to God.[5]

To contemporary ears some sixteenth-century confessional statements sound excessive. This is the case in the discussion of original sin in the *Formula of Concord* when it says, 'That not only is original sin (in human nature) such a complete lack of all good in spiritual, divine matters, but also that at the same time it replaces the lost image of God in the human being with a deep-seated, evil, horrible, bottomless, unfathomable, and indescribable corruption of the entire human nature and all its powers.'[6] This Lutheran interpretation of the fallen state of humans is the starting point of Johann Arndt's early seventeenth-century devotional classic *True Christianity*. Arndt begins by explaining that as humans were created in the image of God, they conformed in all ways with God. But the fall of Adam destroyed the image of God and replaced it with the image of Satan. So Arndt says of humankind, 'In his understanding he was blinded, in his will disobedient and antagonistic to God, in all the powers of his heart he was twisted and became God's enemy.'[7] While many contemporary Lutherans disagree with such strong language about sin and would assert that in some sense the image of God is not lost, they continue to affirm the underlying point that sin involves active resistance to God.

The Mystery of Grace

The counterpoint to human helplessness through sin is the strong Lutheran emphasis on God's gracious initiative as the ground of faith. Faith is entirely God's gift. However, this way of understanding grace raises a difficult question: if faith is a divine gift, why does God not give it to everyone? The popular view that says humans have the sovereign freedom either to accept or refuse God's gift of faith avoids this difficulty by placing the final responsibility for both faith and unfaith on human shoulders. Lutheran teachings acknowledge that humans often have this sort of freedom in matters of this world, but they insist that we do not have it in relation to God. On the other hand, in Lutheran teaching, God does not compel people: they can refuse grace. The important point is that refusing grace is not a truly free act. It is like the young girl Beth refusing to trust you or anyone else. Her refusal to trust simply continues the bondage of distrust. It is similar to an alcoholic's refusal to receive treatment. The refusal is really another manifestation of the bondage to alcohol. In similar fashion, to refuse grace is to persist in idolatrous distrust, and is not a genuinely free act. In this way Lutheran teaching tries to steer a course between free choice and compulsion. Only God is able to evoke the new response of faith.

But then questions come up: Why does God not evoke the response of faith in everyone? Why is it that some have faith and not others? Like Augustine long before, Luther and the *Formula of Concord* appeal to predestination as part of their answer. The doctrine of predestination teaches that, prior to anything any human has done, God has chosen the elect for salvation. But this doctrine only provides part of the answer, because it invites the further question: How does God decide who will or will not receive faith? Luther and the Lutheran Confessions reply, 'We cannot know the answer to such questions, for these matters belong to the hidden, unrevealed counsels of God. Rather, we should fasten our attention on what God has revealed, namely, divine mercy in Jesus Christ and the declaration that God "desires everyone to be saved and to come to the knowledge of the truth", 1 Timothy 2:4.' In effect, when the question arises, 'Why doesn't God give faith to everyone?', the answer of Luther and the Confessions is to say finally, 'We don't know. God is beyond our understanding.' As a result, in the Lutheran tradition the doctrine of predestination never occupied as central a place as it did in the Reformed tradition. The key concerns have been the bondage of sin and the gift of freedom through God's gracious initiative.

Implications for Spiritual Practice

Those Lutherans who take seriously their confessional tradition on sin, free will, and grace may have objections to some

approaches to Christian spiritual practice, as may be illustrated by the following three examples.

1. A very common way of understanding the divine–human
encounter is the popular view that portrays God making an
offer of salvation that people are free to accept or refuse. The
decision to accept Jesus 'into my heart' or 'as my Saviour' is
then made central to becoming a Christian. Indeed, it is
common to ask, 'When did you become a Christian?' and to
expect an answer that tells when the person made that great
decision. The focus of the drama of salvation is on our decision
rather than on where it belongs – God's grace.

To be sure, the element of human decision should not be
totally discounted. In the religious experience of many, a
moment of decision is crucial. The challenge of Joshua to the
ancient Israelites is relevant to later generations also, 'Choose
this day whom you will serve' (Joshua 24:15). Nevertheless,
primary attention in preaching, teaching, and mission work
should be given to God's prior grace that lays the foundation
for any human choice of God.

2. Lutherans have also had questions about some understandings of asceticism. For instance, Methodist Robin Maas
and Roman Catholic Gabriel O'Donnell say, 'Ascetical theology
is concerned with the efforts we as free and responsible
individuals have to make to prepare for the visitation of God',
and 'Ascetical theology deals with the efforts we all must make
to get ready for God.'[8] Another example is the method of
Anthony de Mello who speaks of having found it relatively
easy to teach people to pray, and indeed to help them find
satisfaction and fulfilment in prayer, through using an
approach suggested by a Hindu guru. This approach begins
with sitting for ten minutes with eyes closed in silence. Silence,
he teaches, is the great revelation, and even a person whose
thoughts wander has a minimal silence within.

> It is this minimal silence that you have within you that we
> shall build on in the exercises that follow. As it grows it
> will reveal to you more and more about yourself. Or, more

accurately, silence will reveal yourself to you. That is its first revelation: your *self*. And in and through this revelation you will attain things that money cannot buy, things like wisdom and serenity and joy and God.

To attain these priceless things it is not enough for you to reflect, talk, discuss. What you will need is work. Get to work right now.[9]

The approach of this book is troubling to Lutherans. It suggests that finding God is a matter of human spiritual management, and finding the right meditation technique is the key. Therefore, it's vital to work hard at perfecting the right technique. So the title of the book puts the focus on that technique as the way to God. Whereas Scripture puts the accent on grace, on God's coming to people, de Mello begins by stressing our coming to God through a certain meditation technique.

So how should the body and breath exercises that de Mello uses be viewed from a Lutheran perspective? Luther's own response to various religious practices of his day is instructive. He rejected those practices which he thought contradicted faith in the gospel, but for the most part he objected to false opinions about devotional practices. The latter is the appropriate way of handling de Mello's exercises. Many people have found the breath and body exercises used by de Mello and others helpful, and their Christian faith has been deepened thereby. The problem does not lie with the bodily exercises, but with some of the teaching associated with them. De Mello's way of presenting these exercises should be critiqued, because it detracts from the gospel message of God's gracious initiative and instead encourages a human-centred effort to reach God. This issue of asceticism is one to which we will return later in the book.

3. Lutherans are likely to question also some ideas that accompany the Jesuit method of attending to one's deepest desire. According to this, each one of us has a multitude of desires, but to discern one's deepest desire is to discover one's

desire for God and one's own true self. Philip Sheldrake gives a thoughtful rendering of this approach:

> Discernment may be thought of as a journey through desires – a process whereby we move from a multitude of desires, or from surface desires, to our deepest desire which, as it were, *contains* all that is true and vital about ourselves.
>
> This is a process of inclusion rather than exclusion. The movement inward is where the essential self, or image of God within, may be encountered. Yet this journey also involves engaging with the ambiguities of desire. Initially we are aware of many, sometimes contradictory desires. How are we to recognize the level of deepest desire that truly includes all that we *are*? For the mystics Meister Eckhart and Julian of Norwich that which is evil or destructive or sinful, and which is excluded, is in the end nothing, 'no-thing.' All that is good and has meaning is part of what we mean by deepest desire because it is part of ourselves and part of God. At the heart of all of us is a center that is a point of intersection where our deepest desire and God's desiring in us meet and are found to coincide.[10]

The first time I encountered this teaching was in a lecture given by a Jesuit at a Catholic retreat centre, and I remember gathering during the break with a couple of other Lutherans in the audience to share our doubts about this approach. What were our doubts? Note that what is evil or sinful is in the end nothing, 'no-thing'. In other words, this is a privation theory of sin. Sin is not so much the distortion or corruption of what is good as the loss of certain good qualities. Untouched by this loss is the deepest human desire, which is the desire both for God and for our own true self; indeed, this deepest desire is our own authentic being. A Lutheran understanding of the human condition is somewhat more negative. Every human power suffers distortion, and humans are viewed as being more actively resistant to God. Humans not only lack trust in God, they *distrust* their creator. In this outlook there is no pure human core untouched by sin.

Lutherans can agree with Augustine's confession to God that 'Thou has formed us for Thyself, and our hearts are restless till they find rest in Thee.'[11] That is, the very structure of our being is oriented toward God, so that we can find true fulfilment only in communion with God. However, this ontological structure does not require that there be some existential area of the human make-up which is unaffected by the disorientation of sin.

This is not to deny that empirically the Jesuit approach to discernment is often very helpful. From a Lutheran perspective, the practice of discerning one's desires is not objectionable, but only some of the teaching associated with the practice. In a Lutheran outlook, the usefulness of sorting through one's many desires and affirming one's deep desire for God comes from the fact that God's grace is already at work in the discernment situation. Even though someone might come to a spiritual director with no explicit faith in God, the very act of coming is grounded in God's prior call.[12]

3. JUSTIFICATION BY GRACE THROUGH FAITH

There is broad agreement among Christians that the foundation of human well-being is right relation with God. Even as they believe the most basic feature of the human predicament is alienation from God, so they hold the most fundamental element in human healing is right relation with God. Yet there are variations in the way Christian traditions understand how right relation with God comes about. The Lutheran tradition teaches that it comes about through justification by grace alone through faith alone. In fact, the Lutheran Confessions say the doctrine of justification is the central criterion for all Christian teaching and practice. Lutherans recognize that Scripture also uses others metaphors to speak of salvation such as the movement from alienation to reconciliation, from darkness to light, from death to life, and from bondage to freedom. Yet the metaphor of justification drawn from the ancient legal system is favoured by Paul and is crucial for a full understanding of God's work of salvation in Jesus Christ.

All major Christian traditions teach that justification is by grace, but there is some divergence in how this is interpreted. Focusing on the meaning of 'grace' illuminates the first significant difference. Martin Luther distinguished two main aspects of grace – God's favour and God's gift. God's *favour* is acceptance of the sinner, being favourable toward the sinner; it's often expressed as forgiveness of sin. The other aspect of grace is God's *gift* or gifts that transform a person. God gives gifts such as faith in God, love toward others, hope in difficult circumstances, and patience under trials. So God's grace includes both forgiveness and transformation. On these points, all major Christian traditions agree.

Differences appear, though, when we look closer. In most Christian traditions transformative grace is primary. For instance, in the Orthodox, Roman Catholic, Methodist, and revivalistic Evangelical communities, the chief accent falls on the grace that transforms. God's favour or forgiveness is also acknowledged, but the focus is more on grace that renews and makes holy. So it is that in Orthodoxy and Roman Catholicism veneration of saints is a prominent practice, for saints are recognized by these communities as inspiring examples of divine transformation at work. In Methodist or Wesleyan churches holiness and perfection have been prominent themes. In revivalistic Evangelical circles forgiveness is commonly treated early in the order of salvation, but sanctification receives more attention as the centrality of the born-again experience indicates.

In contrast, the Lutheran Confessions place primary emphasis on God's favour or forgiveness. In dealing with pastoral questions about repentance and his own religious struggle to have peace with God, Martin Luther found the solid ground of certainty in God's merciful acceptance of the sinner. He pressed the question, how can we be sure that we are in right relation with God? Luther believed that in this life on earth the Christian is always a mix of new and old, faith and unfaith, love and selfishness. Even saints recognized as models of holiness still have elements of sin in their lives. So God's gracious work of transformation is always incomplete in this life. Because the Christian on earth is always a mix of righteousness and sin, the only secure basis for peace with God is divine favour that forgives and accepts. Out of God's mercy for Christ's sake, the believer is *declared righteous*. Because this being declared righteous suggests a divine court-room, it is often called *forensic justification*.

It's not that Luther recognizes only the aspect of divine favour, for he affirms that transforming grace is also always at work in believers. Through the Holy Spirit the believer is also *made righteous*. However, since transforming grace bears only partial fruit in this life, that fruit is not a basis for one's acceptance before God. Luther's concern is this: if holiness coming even from grace were the decisive factor for being right with God, then people would look at their own holiness and wonder whether they had enough. They could never be sure of having sufficient holiness. The bedrock of the believer's relationship with God is the divine favour that forgives and accepts. So one important difference in the understanding of justification by grace is the relative weight and significance given to transforming grace or forgiving grace, and the Lutheran Confessions' primary emphasis on forgiving grace is exceptional among Christian traditions.

A second important point regarding justification by grace is that the Lutheran Confessions teach that justification is by *grace alone*. This was the case also for Augustine and Thomas Aquinas. However, a number of late medieval theologians held that while God takes the initiative in bestowing grace, humans contribute also to salvation by virtue of free will even independently of grace.[1] Luther and the Lutheran Confessions insisted that justification is by grace alone. The Council of Trent took a position close to the grace alone view of Thomas Aquinas rather than the late medieval nominalist theologians. Trent said Christians should trust in God, not in themselves, yet they are judged 'not apart from' the merits given them by grace.[2]

A third difference has been over the role of faith in justification. Lutherans have taught justification by grace through *faith alone*. The Council of Trent said that faith is the essential beginning of salvation, but insisted that faith is not living unless hope and love are added to it. This divergence is caused in part by different definitions of faith. On the Catholic side, faith was understood chiefly as assent to something as true. In this sense, even the demons have faith, for they believe God is one. So Catholic theologians insisted that living faith is formed by love and manifest in good works (James 2:14-26).

On the Lutheran side, faith was understood as trust in God's promise of mercy on account of Christ. This faith is a work of the Holy Spirit who converts the will, so faith is a work of transforming grace. It's clear that faith in Christ is not just subjective, but is a profound relationship with the triune God that is marked by deep trust and devotion. Such faith is inherently active in resisting sin and doing good. As *Augsburg Confession* Article 6 says, 'It is also taught that such faith should yield good fruit and good works and that a person must do such good works as God has commanded for God's sake but not place trust in them as if thereby to earn grace before God.'

Concern to distinguish clearly between forgiving grace and transforming grace led authors of the *Formula of Concord* (1577) to make a sharper distinction in terminology. In the Formula justification is limited to forgiving grace and transforming grace is generally called sanctification. This distinction between justification and sanctification became standard usage in Lutheranism. The terminological distinction, though, tended to reduce awareness of the unity of these two dimensions of God's gracious activity.

Later Developments

Although the accent fell on forgiving grace during the foundational years of Lutheranism, during the seventeenth century Lutherans associated with Pietism put the primary accent on transforming grace. There were at least two reasons for this shift. One was the quality of life in many Lutheran churches. In the early years when very few bishops supported the Lutheran reform movement, Luther looked to the civil rulers to lead church reform. Over time this emergency measure turned out to have negative consequences. Many princes used the church to maintain civil order and to further their own ends. Virtually everyone within a territory was baptized, and princes often imposed laws requiring attendance at worship. People heard the message of justification by faith, but many did not experience the relationship with Christ that it was meant to foster; they took it as blanket approval of an unchanged life. A second reason for the Pietist shift was Lutheran Orthodox theology which was highly rational, usually couched in the language of Aristotle's philosophy, and very polemical. Such theology often failed to nurture faith and tended to promote conflict and a clergy separated from their people.

Johann Arndt, the grandfather of Pietism, responded by calling for a reduction in theological polemics among the clergy, but also more centrally for living faith. The opening words of his Foreword to *True Christianity* (1610) are these:

> Dear Christian reader, that the holy Gospel is subjected, in our time, to a great and shameful abuse is fully proved by the impenitent life of the ungodly who praise Christ and his word with their mouths and yet lead an unchristian life that is like that of persons who dwell in heathendom, not in the Christian world. Such ungodly conduct gave me cause to write this book to show simple readers wherein true Christianity consists, namely, in the exhibition of a true, living faith, active in genuine godliness and the fruits of righteousness. [I wished to show as well] that we bear the name of Christ, not only because we ought to believe in Christ, but also because we are to live in Christ and he in us. [I also wished to show] how true repentance must proceed from the innermost source of the heart; how the heart, mind, and affections must be changed, so that we might be conformed to Christ and his holy Gospel; and how we must be renewed by the word of God to become new creatures.[3]

Although Arndt thinks his historical context calls for a primary emphasis on transforming grace, he urges this in such a way as to maintain the Lutheran confessional stance that justification is by grace alone and faith alone. He says,

> You must take care that you do not connect your works and the virtues that you have begun, or the gifts of the

new life, with your justification before God, for none of
man's works, merit, gifts, or virtue, however lovely these
may be, count for anything. [Our justification depends] on
the exalted, perfect merit of Jesus Christ, received by
faith . . . Take great care, therefore, not to confound the
righteousness of faith with the righteousness of a
Christian life, but make a clear distinction [between
them], for here is the whole foundation of our Christian
religion.[4]

Arndt shifts the emphasis to transforming grace by stressing
– like Luther – that faith is a living and active reality and that
by faith we live in Christ and Christ lives in us. So faith in
Christ is a personal relationship with Christ marked by deep
trust and commitment to his way of life. In contrast to the
dominant concern of the Orthodox for maintaining the objective truth of Lutheran doctrine, Arndt is chiefly concerned
with the experiential impact of Christian teaching. So in his
opening words, he wishes to show 'how the heart, mind, and
affections must be changed'. Many of Arndt's concerns were
shared by others who are often designated the reform party
within Lutheranism. These include Joachim Luetkemann
(1608–55), Henry Mueller (1631–75), and Christian Scriver
(1629–93), all of whom wrote popular devotional works. The
need for reform was heightened by the Thirty Years' War
(1618–48), which caused extensive damage to life, property,
and moral fabric in many German territories.

   The Arndtian reform tradition's stress on transforming
grace or sanctification was continued and given organizational
structure by the Pietist movement led by Philip Jacob Spener
(1635–1705) and his successor August Hermann Francke
(1663–1727). While they affirmed that new life is grounded in
God's grace, Spener and Francke also stressed that the individual must respond to that grace and strive for holiness.
Francke went through a definite inner struggle and conversion experience, which he considered is God's usual way with
people, but he did not make it a rigid norm or employ methods

to bring it about as in later revivalism. Like Pietists from the Reformed tradition of Calvin and the Puritans, Spener to some extent but especially Francke gave detailed rules for Christian conduct. This contributed to a puritanical and legalistic spirit in many Pietist circles.

Nevertheless, both Spener and Francke regarded themselves as genuine Lutherans. This assessment of Francke by scholar of Pietism F. Ernest Stoeffler could be applied also to Spener:

> [Francke] thought of himself as being essentially Lutheran. As such he adhered to Luther's Christo-centrism and to the Reformer's basic insights concerning sin, justification, the means of grace etc. All of this was modified, however, insofar as he understood Luther through the Arndtian tradition. Whether or not this can be called 'a thoroughgoing transformation' of Luther's basic theological insights is a matter of interpretation. Perhaps it would be more accurate to speak of a new emphasis, which in part is the result of the Arndtian influence, and in part the result of a changed historical situation.[5]

After the heyday of Pietism the meaning of justification and the relation between forgiving grace and transforming grace have persisted as core concerns among Lutherans. In the nineteenth century Neo-Lutheranism renewed interest in Luther and the Lutheran Confessions with their focus on justification, and this was continued by many Lutheran theologians in the twentieth century. During Hitler's rise to power Dietrich Bonhoeffer coined two terms that have become commonplace in popular discussions of justification – cheap grace and costly grace. Cheap grace is proclaiming forgiveness without repentance and discipleship to Jesus; it is claiming forgiving grace apart from transforming grace. Only costly grace is genuinely God's grace, for it involves both forgiveness and transformation.[6]

Because of its centrality for Lutherans, the doctrine of

justification has been a critical issue in their ecumenical discussions. Several ecumenical dialogues between Lutheran and Roman Catholic theologians laid the foundation for the *Joint Declaration on the Doctrine of Justification* signed by the Lutheran World Federation and the Roman Catholic Church in 1999. This document expresses a consensus on the basic truths of justification and says the remaining differences on this topic are no longer grounds for doctrinal condemnations. It says, 'Together we confess: By grace alone, in faith in Christ's saving work and not because of any merit on our part, we are accepted by God and receive the Holy Spirit, who renews our hearts while equipping and calling us to good works.'[7] There is agreement that justification is by grace alone. The difference of emphasis on justification as declaring righteous and making righteous remains, but they agree, 'These two aspects of God's gracious action are not to be separated, for persons are by faith united with Christ, who in his person is our righteousness . . .'[8] Another remaining difference is whether it is fully appropriate to speak of justification by faith *alone*, but both parties agree on two key points: such faith is active in love and 'whatever in the justified precedes or follows the free gift of faith is neither the basis of justification nor merits it.'[9]

Dialogues between Eastern Orthodox and Lutheran theologians have occurred in several contexts, but the dialogue in Finland has spurred a new school of Luther research, which sees a larger place for transforming grace and claims that Luther affirms the Orthodox concern for *theosis,* divinization, wherein the believer participates in the qualities of God.[10] Not all Luther scholars fully agree. For instance, Erich Gritsch says, 'Justification thus leads to "Christ-ification", as it were, to cohabitation, by faith, with Christ. When, then, Luther speaks of sanctification, he can say that the Holy Spirit makes a Christian "holy" (*geheiligt*), but this must happen in a daily struggle between sin and grace.' So while their thought overlaps to some extent, Luther's strong emphasis on daily struggle distinguishes his thought from the Orthodox notion of divinization.[11]

Justification by Faith and Spiritual Practice

The *Augsburg Confession* (1530) makes it clear that justification by grace through faith alone has implications for spiritual practice. The Confession is divided into two parts, the first dealing with articles of faith and doctrine, the second with practices that the Lutherans considered abuses. Among the latter were several practices that they believed conflicted with justification by faith. Endowed and private masses were rejected in large part on the grounds that people believed they would gain merit with God not by faith in Christ, but by performing the work of the mass. A similar objection was raised to the teaching that observing certain days, fasts, and monastic vows were useful works for meriting grace. In many cases, the objection was not to the practices as such, but to what were considered false opinions about them. So in the *Augsburg Confession* Lutherans insist that they celebrate the mass, although not privately, and they encourage observance of holy days and fasting. Even monastic vows are not ruled out, for the voluntary vows in Augustine's time are positively contrasted to later imposed requirements.

One prominent difference from Orthodox and Roman Catholic practice is that Lutherans do not pray to saints. This is related to justification by faith, for it is faith in Jesus Christ that counts. Lutherans remember saints with gratitude both individually and liturgically, and quite a few Lutheran churches are named after saints, although mostly New Testament figures. But they do not pray to Mary or other saints, because they are worried that this implies relying upon someone besides Christ for salvation.

The concern that spiritual practice be consistent with justification by faith has been persistent throughout the history of Lutheranism. As we have noted, Lutheran Pietists argued that their practice was in harmony with this central doctrine. The concern is apparent also today. For instance, American Luther scholar James Kittleson finds fault with three recent books on spirituality by Lutherans, his chief criticism being that they are synergistic. Kittleson argues that they violate the principle of grace alone by importing human initiative into the God–human relationship through the back door. In contrast, he says, Luther presents a model of a rigorous spirituality grounded thoroughly on grace alone and faith alone.[12]

At its best, the Lutheran tradition's focus on the *doctrine* of justification by faith has had the underlying purpose of fostering a certain kind of *relationship* with Christ. Martin Luther describes this relationship in *The Freedom of a Christian* when he explains the powerful nature of faith by identifying its three elements: faith trusts and clings to the promises of God; faith honours and reveres God from the heart; and faith unites the believer with Christ like a bride is united with her bridegroom.[13] Luther scholar Scott Hendrix says Luther's reformation of spirituality is 'the connectedness of Christians to Christ which they have not chosen but instead received'.[14] In this faith relationship, the believer is *free from* the neverending quest to earn good standing with God, and at the same time *free for* service to God and others.

The believer's close faith relationship with Christ is a recurrent theme in the tradition. Lutheran Orthodox theologian Johann Gerhard says faith unites believers to the Saviour as branches draw their sustenance from the vine (John 15:4).[15] Later Lutheran Orthodox theologians commonly spoke of an order of salvation which included mystical union with Christ or the triune God as an aspect of salvation simultaneous with faith and justification.[16] Faith union with Christ is also dear to the Pietists. In their own ways Spener and Francke followed Johann Arndt's strong accent on transforming grace in the believer by Christ's presence in the believer through faith. Spener focused on the practical effects of the present Christ on the believer's will to follow him. Francke stressed the experiential impact of Christ and the Holy Spirit on the believer's heart.[17] Fellowship with Christ in faith is an essential feature of costly grace and Christian discipleship for Bonhoeffer: 'Cheap grace is grace without discipleship, grace without the cross, grace without Jesus Christ, living and incarnate.'[18]

Lutherans and Mysticism

With such emphasis on close relationship and union with Christ, are these Lutherans mystics? Much depends on how one defines 'mystic' and 'mysticism'. Bernard McGinn is helpful in making a distinction between mystical elements and mysticism proper or explicit mysticism. He says there are mystical elements expressed in New Testament passages such as Paul's affirmation, 'it is no longer I who live, but it is Christ who lives in me' (Gal. 2:20) and John's words, 'Abide in me as I abide in you. Just as the branch cannot bear fruit by itself unless it abides in the vine, neither can you unless you abide in me' (John 15:4).

McGinn says, 'The great tradition of explicit mysticism came to birth when a theory of mysticism first fully laid out by Origen in the third century found institutional embodiment in the new phenomenon of monasticism in the fourth century.'[19] Origen's theory of mysticism distinguishes three stages which were later designated by Pseudo-Dionysius as purgation, illumination, and union with God. This spiritual movement consists centrally in the redirection of one's love/eros/desire, from inordinate love of creatures to love of God and ultimately ecstatic possession of God. Origen stressed pure sexual abstinence as the preferred path for mystical practice. The spiritual movement also involves changes in one's knowledge of God, changes that go from affirmation of divine qualities to negation of those qualities and then, for Dionysius, to the negation of negation. Pseudo-Dionysius has a thoroughly apophatic theology in which the highest knowing of God is unknowing. This whole spiritual movement is the process of divinization whereby persons participate in the being of God.[20] McGinn goes on in later volumes to trace the development of other forms of mysticism, yet much of the foundation of western Christian mysticism is laid by Origen and Pseudo-Dionysius.

So what about Lutherans and mysticism? Surely there are mystical elements present in Lutheranism. Luther and many others resonate deeply to John's vine and branches image and Paul's affirmations of believers being in Christ and Christ in believers. In addition, Paul's understanding of baptism as dying and rising with Christ plays a central role in Lutheran practice and self-understanding.

Yet Lutherans have regarded representatives of mysticism proper with mixed assessments. Luther thought explicit mysticism and monastic practice closely associated with it were often pervaded with works righteousness that did not rely fully on God's grace in Christ. In his view Pseudo-Dionysius is, 'Downright dangerous, for he is more of a Platonist than a Christian. So if I had my way, no believing soul would give the least attention to these books. So far, indeed, from learning Christ in them, you will lose even what you already know of him.'[21] Also in contrast to the widely accepted Dionysian idea that union with God is the experience of a relative few in the final stage of spiritual ascent, Luther democratized the notion by teaching that faith in Christ intrinsically involves union with Christ. On the other hand, he praised Bernard of Clairvaux and Johann Tauler, both prominent mystics, and published the anonymous mystical work *German Theology*. Yet Luther was always highly selective in what he affirmed about the mystics he knew. He affirmed the Christ-centredness of Bernard. He valued the utter dependence on God found in Tauler and the *German Theology*, and he appreciated that they spoke out of their experience rather than spinning out theoretical ideas like the scholastic theologians.[22]

Many Lutheran Pietists found some medieval mystics congenial, but they also sought to set aside elements in them that conflicted with justification by grace through faith alone. Johann Arndt republished the *German Theology*, and in his own *True Christianity* borrowed freely from texts by mystical writers, especially Angela of Foligno and Tauler. When he was attacked for his use of mystical sources, Arndt acknowledged that some of these authors 'may seem to ascribe more than is due to human ability and works, but my whole book strives against such [an error].' He insisted that 'All must be drawn from Christ, the wellspring, through faith', and urged readers not to confuse their always incomplete righteousness from transforming grace with the complete righteousness ascribed to the believer through forgiveness.[23] Philip Spener also adopted a selectively positive attitude toward several mystical writers. He appreciated that they were not interested in mere speculative knowledge, but touched the heart. He noted two main reservations – reliance on human achievement that conflicts with justification by faith and the 'enthusiastic' teaching of union with God apart from any external Word or sacrament. Spener wrote:

> A pious reader will discover thoughts, counsels, and observations in the works of Tauler, Kempis, Gerson, the author of the *German Theology*, and other writers of this kind of book. Their style of writing . . . does move and grasp the heart. Anything that is in these books which arises out of the papal filth and the errors ascribed to Platonism can be noted and avoided without difficulty by anyone who understands our true doctrine.[24]

Although they do not speak directly about mysticism, two contemporary Lutherans have different assessments of some core convictions and practices closely linked with it in Christian history. On the rather negative side, James Kittleson criticizes three recent Lutheran spiritual writers for offering a watered-down version of monastic piety focused on brief times of silence and solitude, withdrawn from daily life, rather than Luther's spirituality that is centred in service to others in the relationships of daily life.[25] On a more positive side, David Yeago, another American, approves at least one major feature of mysticism proper. As Bernard McGinn indicated, Origen and Pseudo-Dionysius conceived the fundamental spiritual movement as one of redirection of love/eros/desire from creatures to

loving God above all things. This movement is basic also for
Augustine as well as for Thomas Merton. David Yeago considers that much Lutheran suspicion of spirituality is based on
the belief that the endeavour of classical Christian spirituality to reorder our desire conflicts with justification by faith.
Yeago argues that this suspicion rests on a mistaken understanding of justification. In his 'prolegomena to a Lutheran
retrieval of classical spiritual theology', he emphasizes that
the content of the gospel promise affirmed by Luther and the
Lutheran Confessions is Jesus Christ living and present. This
living and present Christ brings both forgiveness and change
in desires. So Yeago says, 'The questions about desire at the
heart of that tradition may now be seen as uniquely *appropriate* questions for a spiritual theology built on the
Reformation gospel.'[26]

This positive perspective on classical Christian spirituality
is reflected in the 1998 Lutheran Theological Southern
Seminary faculty position paper 'Spirituality and Spiritual
Formation', whose chief drafter was Yeago. The position paper
says Luther 'drew heavily on patristic and medieval pastoral
and monastic resources' and regards the great Lutheran spiritual writers of Pietism and Orthodoxy as remarkably
ecumenical. It concludes, 'Today also Lutheran spirituality is
an essentially ecumenical endeavor. Our task is to engage and
integrate the classical Christian tradition and the best contemporary resources in a theologically and pastorally
responsible fashion.'[27]

Image of the Christian Life

Roman Catholic authors Lawrence Cunningham and Keith
Egan identify three influential maps or images of the
Christian life – journey, ascent, and human development. The
dominant image of the Christian life in Christian mysticism
has been ascent to God in the same way that Moses ascended
Mount Sinai to receive God's revelation. While this image can
be combined with journey, human development to maturity, or

other metaphors, both Origen and Pseudo-Dionysius concentrate on ascent to God by redirection of desire and deepening of knowledge through three stages. In both writers the ascent takes place within the context of a Christian community and its worship.[28]

What, then, is the dominant image of the Christian life in Lutheran spirituality? The ascent image encounters considerable resistance among Lutherans, who affirm that Christians are, in Luther's terms, always *simul iustus et peccator*, at the same time righteous and sinner. This idea has been difficult for Roman Catholic theologians to accept. Indeed, this was the first item on a list of eight rejected by the Vatican in its initial response to the *Joint Declaration on the Doctrine of Justification* prior to its eventual acceptance by both parties.

The image of the Christian life that has appeared often among Lutherans is dying and rising with Christ. Generations of Lutherans have learned Luther's *Small Catechism* explanation of baptism, 'It signifies that the old creature in us with all sins and evil desires is to be drowned and die through daily contrition and repentance, and on the other hand that daily a new person is to come forth and rise up to live before God in righteousness and purity forever.'[29] This focus on daily dying and rising with Christ might suggest a picture of the Christian life in which the Christian is always running on the same spot. These words of Luther seem to support this picture, 'To advance is always a matter of beginning anew.'[30]

Yet the biblical image of journey implies some movement forward, and Paul's image of human development toward maturity implies advancement or growth. In an effort to affirm some growth in the Christian life, at times Arndt draws on the Dionysian three-stage view of the Christian path – purgation, illumination, and union with God. He says:

> Just as our natural life has its steps, namely, childhood, manhood, and old age, so also does our spiritual and Christian life. It, too, has its beginnings in repentance, by which man daily betters himself. Thereafter follows

middle age, more illumination, through the contemplation of divine things, through prayer, and through suffering. By all of these the gifts of God are increased. Finally, the perfection of old age comes. It consists in the full union through love . . .[31]

Arndt also distinguishes three kinds of prayer that in the tradition of mysticism are often correlated with the three stages of the Christian life – oral prayer, internal prayer or meditation, and supernatural prayer. He says:

According to Tauler, "consists in a true union with God by faith; when our created spirit dissolves, as it were, and sinks away in the uncreated Spirit of God. It is then that all is transacted in a moment, which in words or deeds has been done by all the saints from the beginning of the world."[32]

Arndt qualifies his use of the three stages by emphasizing that sin remains in Christians and that they always need to repent and rely on Christ.

Rather than incorporating the three-stages scheme of purgation, illumination, and union, a better approach for Lutherans is to delve more deeply into the image of dying and rising with Christ. If we acknowledge the truth in human experience that the biblical images of journey and maturation illuminate, we will see that being in Christ is not just running on the same spot. There is movement in this relationship akin to what happens in a marriage relationship over time. A marriage relationship has ups and downs. Over time it can deteriorate and end in divorce. It can stay on a relatively superficial level. Or it can also grow and deepen. My wife and I have been married over forty years now. I don't think I love my wife 'more' than on our wedding day, but there is no doubt that our love has deepened and matured over time. The relevant question is not so much how I have grown individually in this quality of love, but how our relationship has deepened.

And it has deepened through renewing our commitment and sharing experiences, thoughts, and feelings through the years.

Similarly, daily dying and rising with Christ is not just like running on the same spot or never getting beyond square one. This daily dynamic of turning to Christ in faith involves the movement into a deeper relationship with Christ. So it's never a matter of checking the degree of one's individual holiness. The relationship is what counts. Thus, the image of dying and rising with Christ can and should be combined with the biblical images of journey and human development.[33] God does work in and through the events of our lives to move believers closer to maturity in Christ. Even the image of ascent up the mountain may have a place for Lutherans, because just as in the church year there is both Transfiguration and Easter, so in the Christian life there are both ecstatic moments and moments of suffering. Although Lutherans can and should acknowledge and value the peak religious experiences, they do not consider that such moments should be the centre of attention. Luther rejected a theology of glory in favour of a theology of the cross. So while some Christian traditions focus on experiences of power and victory, Lutherans emphasize that God meets us most profoundly in suffering and the cross. If the image of ascent suggests a picture of a gradual upward line, a Lutheran picture of the Christian life would be more like a horizontal spiral moving forward, ever further into faith's mystery of being in Christ. The movement forward is around Christ as centre, and it penetrates ever deeper into the darkness of life. This is a picture suggested by a relationship with God in which we are justified by grace alone through faith alone.

4. AUTHORITY AND SOURCES OF WISDOM

It is common to address the issue of authority in theology, but one might wonder what it has to do with spirituality. Much depends on the meaning of both spirituality and authority.

I have suggested this definition of spirituality: a faith with a path. The path is a set of practices that both express and nurture the particular faith. A good way of stating much the same thing in sentence form is this: spirituality is intentional practice of a particular faith.[1] In both formulations spirituality involves practices related to a certain faith. In addition to elements of commitment, trust, and hope, faith includes a view of human life and of the world. So the practices that express and nurture this faith are intimately connected with a particular outlook on reality. To think about faith and especially its view of life and the world is to be engaged in theological reflection, and the product of this activity is a theology. Every spirituality is closely linked with a corresponding theology.[2] So the authorities adhered to in this theology will also shape the spirituality. However, the way in which authority functions in spirituality may be less obvious than in theology.

The nature of authority in theology and spirituality needs to be clarified, for there are different kinds of authority. For instance, recently I heard a reporter on BBC radio say that 'the authorities' in Australia were moving people out of an urban area threatened by a spreading forest fire. Most likely these authorities were law enforcement personnel appointed by various civil entities. Such civic authorities are given power to maintain a certain order by enforcing laws and protecting human life and property. The authority given to police includes at least in certain circumstances the power to force others to obey.

The relation between spiritual communities and civil authorities with police power has varied over time. In sixteenth-century Europe the police power of civil authority had great influence on what spiritualities were permitted or proscribed in a given territory. As we have seen, in 1520 Martin Luther was brought before the Holy Roman Emperor at Worms, and soon declared an outlaw. Luther's views would have won few followers without the protection and support of some princes. The primary Lutheran statement, the *Augsburg Confession*, although written by theologians, was signed by princes. War erupted between princes, and the Lutheran movement was nearly crushed before a military resurgence led to the Peace of Augsburg (1555) and agreement that a prince had the right to establish either Catholicism or Lutheranism in his territory. Later the terrible Thirty Years' War (1618–48) was fought over religion, and in most parts of Europe particular forms of spirituality were favoured or limited by civil authority until the twentieth century. So while civil police authority is in many respects external to Lutheran spirituality, the opportunities for expression and growth of Lutheran faith and practice have been greatly determined by civil powers. This has been true not only in Europe, but also in many other lands colonized by Europeans. Just as predominance of Roman Catholicism in Latin America is rooted in Spanish and Portuguese colonial power, so a strong Lutheran Church in Namibia today was born out of German colonialism.

While spiritual communities seldom have their own police to enforce rulings physically, they generally have judicatories to keep order in the community. For example, almost every church body has a person or group with the authority to remove a pastor from office. Yet power to maintain a certain order is not the only kind of authority.

We also speak of someone as an authority on Beethoven or Indonesian history or traditional dance in West Africa. Such influence comes from knowledge and prestige. This is closer to the kind of authority that operates in theology and spirituality. Still closer is authority that comes from wisdom. Wisdom includes knowledge and understanding of truth significant for life, but it also has a strong moral dimension of sound judgement and right use of knowledge. In theology and spirituality a person, group, or writing gains authority by being a reservoir of wisdom for a community. What happens over time in any community of spirituality, religious or not, is that certain persons, groups, or writings are recognized by the community as authoritative. This communal recognition can be formal or informal. If the recognition is formal, then reliance upon and appeals to this authority become accepted procedure in the community.

Lutheran theology and spirituality are primarily shaped by two formally recognized authorities as sources of wisdom – Scripture and the Lutheran Confessions, the ancient creeds and sixteenth-century confessional documents in the *Book of Concord*. Scripture is the primary authoritative source of wisdom, the Lutheran Confessions secondary. A third category of authority is broader church tradition, which includes ancient church practices, decrees of church councils other than those in the *Book of Concord*, and writings of respected earlier theologians.

Scripture alone is a core affirmation of the Lutheran Reformation, in addition to grace alone, faith alone, and Christ alone. However, s*ola Scriptura* does not mean that Scripture is the only authority, but that it is the primary or chief authority to which all others are subordinate. Although the Lutheran Confessions do not have a separate article on the primacy of Scripture, it is assumed throughout in the argumentation. The most explicit statement is given in the preface to the *Formula of Concord* (1577). Here the Bible is said to be 'the only rule and guiding principle according to which all teachings and teachers are to be evaluated and judged'. The preface goes on to confess adherence to the Apostles', Nicene, and Athanasian Creeds and these sixteenth-century documents: the unaltered *Augsburg Confession*, the *Apology of the Augsburg Confession*, the *Smalcald Articles*, and Luther's *Small and Large Catechisms*. The *Augsburg Confession* is the fundamental statement among the later writings, and the others are recognized because they accord with Scripture and the *Augsburg Confession*. These creeds and confessions 'are not judges, as is Holy Scripture, but they are only witnesses and explanations of the faith, which show how Holy Scripture has at various times been understood and interpreted in the church of God by those who lived at the time in regard to articles of faith under dispute . . .'³ Gunther Gassmann and Scott Hendrix point out that this claim includes both doctrine and history. 'Creeds and confessions have authority both because they are grounded in Scripture and because they state the Christian faith in a way both appropriate and necessary for their own time.'⁴ While these specific creeds and confessions are subordinate to Scripture, they in turn have priority over still other authorities that are cited by the Lutheran reformers – practices of the ancient Church, views of earlier theologians, other teachings of church councils, and at times canon law.

Authorities in Lutheran Theology and Spirituality

The relation between Scripture and confessional writings is complex. While in principle Scripture stands above the Lutheran Confessions, the latter express the normative Lutheran way of interpreting Scripture. The *Smalcald Articles* (1537) state this clearly:

Here is the first and chief article:

> That Jesus Christ, our God and Lord, "was handed over to death for our trespasses and was raised for our justification" (Rom. 4[:25]); . . . furthermore, "All have sinned," and "they are now justified without merit by his grace, through the redemption that is in Christ Jesus . . . by his blood" (Rom. 3[:23-25]).
>
> Now because this must be believed and may not be obtained or grasped otherwise with any work, law, or

merit, it is clear and certain that this faith alone justifies us, as St. Paul says in Romans 3[:28, 26] . . .

Nothing in this article can be conceded or given up . . .[5]

This statement that the heart of Scripture is the gospel, the good news of Jesus Christ, and the heart of the gospel is justification by grace alone through faith alone, is what is often called the Lutheran 'canon within the canon'. Since the Bible is a large collection of documents from a diversity of times, places, authors, and editors, it includes a variety of perspectives. Lutherans share with most other Christians the conviction that Jesus Christ is the heart of the whole Bible, for ultimately the Old Testament is also to be understood in light of Christ. However, various Christian traditions of theology and spirituality focus on different aspects of Christ. For Lutherans the core of the gospel is justification by faith alone. This is the interpretive key for understanding Scripture.

Sometimes Luther is praised or condemned for exalting the individual's understanding of the Bible over against corporate, institutional teaching. This is a mistake. To be sure, he did challenge the power structures of the Church, yet it's important to note how he did it. Martin Luther was himself a very capable biblical scholar, and he also was quite knowledgeable in the history of theology and biblical interpretation. He submitted his views to public, scholarly discussion both in oral and written forms. Furthermore, he did not remain an isolated voice, but gained substantial support of his views from many other theologians and lay leaders. This is exemplified in the fact that the fundamental and most widely accepted Lutheran confessional statement, the *Augsburg Confession*, was written not by Luther, but by Melanchthon. Throughout this Confession Scripture is interpreted according to the Lutheran canon within the canon.

What does this do to the claim that Scripture is the highest authority? Has Lutheran church tradition in the form of its Confessions, in fact, taken priority over Scripture? Luther would say that he is not imposing an alien interpretive key upon the Bible, but is simply making explicit the Bible's own centre. This is clear in his preface to the Letter of James. While Luther calls James a good book, he does not regard it as a writing of an apostle for two reasons. First, 'it is flatly against St. Paul and all the rest of Scripture in ascribing justification to works.' Second, while it mentions Christ, it says nothing about his passion, resurrection, or the Spirit of Christ.

> Now it is the office of a true apostle to preach of the Passion and resurrection and office of Christ, and to lay the foundation for faith in him . . . All the genuine sacred books agree in this, that all of them preach and inculcate [*treiben*] Christ. And that is the true test by which to judge all books, when we see whether or not they inculcate Christ . . . Whatever does not teach Christ is not yet apostolic, even though St. Peter or St. Paul does the teaching.[6]

So Lutherans maintain they are just articulating Scripture's own centre – the gospel of Jesus Christ and justification by faith. Because of this focus on the gospel, Lutherans identified themselves as *evangelicals* long before the more recent forms of evangelical Christianity associated with revivalism.

Recent ecumenical discussions between Roman Catholics and Lutherans have framed this question of the central message of Scripture in terms of justification as criterion for teaching and practice. Whereas Lutheran theologians have stressed justification as *the* criterion, Roman Catholic theologians have seen themselves bound by several criteria. The *Joint Declaration on the Doctrine of Justification* (2000) expresses their agreement that the doctrine of justification is 'an indispensable criterion that constantly serves to orient all the teaching and practice of our churches to Christ.'[7] The annex to the Declaration explains that this means no teaching may contradict this criterion.

The most disputed question about biblical interpretation among Lutherans themselves has been inerrancy of the Bible.

Quite often the issue is posed as a difference between those who interpret the Bible literally and those who do not, but this misses the mark. Those who insist on the inerrancy of Scripture do not interpret every passage literally, for they recognize that Scripture is rich with poetry and metaphor. Furthermore, when a literal meaning seems unreasonable, they often will suggest a metaphorical meaning. For example, in the creation story of Genesis 1 a 'day' may be understood as a geological age rather than a literal day. The fundamental issue is whether the Bible is without error in all respects, and a doctrine of complete verbal inspiration is the buttress for inerrancy.[8]

Inerrancy of Scripture was a doctrine developed by Lutheran and Reformed Orthodox theologians in the context of controversy with Roman Catholic theologians. Although Luther was convinced of the reliability of Scripture as witness to Christ, he did not subscribe to biblical inerrancy, as his view of the Letter of James shows. Nevertheless, inerrancy came to prevail among adherents of Lutheran Orthodoxy, and was generally accepted by Lutheran Pietists. When some German scholars became leaders in historical critical study of the Bible in the nineteenth century, the doctrines of inerrancy and verbal inspiration were severely challenged, but not abandoned by most Lutheran theologians. By 1900 some Lutheran theologians were modifying their thinking, but during the first half of the twentieth century many Lutheran synods in the US still had doctrinal statements affirming at least the infallibility of Scripture. After mid century defence of biblical inerrancy and verbal inspiration waned among Lutherans, although it remains a fervently held minority opinion. Fierce conflict over this issue emerged in the Lutheran Church–Missouri Synod in the late 1960s, and those backing inerrancy prevailed. Today the Lutheran Church–Missouri Synod shares this position with several much smaller churches including the Wisconsin Synod in the US, the Independent Evangelical Lutheran Church in Germany, and the Evangelical Lutheran Church of Brazil.

While various forms of historical and literary criticism of the Bible are accepted among most Lutheran theologians, the confessional stance of Scripture's primary authority challenges any approach that does not allow the Bible to speak authoritatively. For instance, some postmodern approaches would insist on the equality of every interpretation.[9] In such a view the biblical text has no authoritative word to speak, but is simply a springboard for anyone's contemporary opinion.

Besides being evangelical with their concentration on the gospel, the Lutherans also claim that their teaching and practice is *catholic* in the sense that it does not contradict universal Christian teaching and practice. Philip Melanchthon especially developed the case for this in the *Augsburg Confession* and the *Apology of the Augsburg Confession*. In support of this claim, for example, Article 1 of the *Augsburg Confession* declares agreement with the Nicene Creed and rejects all heresies opposed to it. A similar approach is employed in most articles of the Confession's first part on doctrine. The conclusion of this first part also says, 'this teaching is clearly grounded in Holy Scripture and is, moreover, neither against nor contrary to the universal Christian church – or even the Roman church – so far as can be observed in the writings of the Fathers.'[10] Then in his conclusion to the whole *Augsburg Confession*, Melanchthon says what is written is intended 'to make it quite clear that among us nothing in doctrine or ceremonies has been accepted that would contradict either Holy Scripture or the universal Christian church'.[11]

The same authorities operate in the realm of practice as in doctrine. The *Augsburg Confession* reflects Lutheran concern for both theology and spiritual practice, for it is divided into two parts – the first called 'Articles of Faith and Doctrine' and the second, longer part entitled 'Disputed Articles, Listing the Abuses That Have Been Corrected'. Both sets of issues are addressed in the context of political and police power, for the *Augsburg Confession* is addressed to the emperor and signed by princes. In the realm of practices also the authoritative sources of wisdom are Scripture, ancient ecumenical creeds, and other ancient traditions all interpreted in light of the gospel core. How these three authoritative sources of wisdom work is evident in the last article of part one concerning the cult of the saints. Veneration of saints had been a widespread practice since ancient times, so Lutherans affirm some form of veneration, namely remembrance of saints as examples. Yet the Confession rejects praying to them for help, because that is contrary to Scripture's witness to Christ as Mediator and Saviour. So ancient tradition is accepted, but certain elements in the tradition are corrected by Scripture interpreted from its gospel core.[12]

These same three authorities operated in Lutheran Reformation spiritual practice, and are evident in practices that are retained, dropped, or modified. This can be seen in corporate worship, devotions, instruction, and institutional life. We will consider these four areas in turn.

Corporate Worship

Luther and those associated with him brought about a relatively conservative reform of corporate worship that included both considerable continuity of received tradition and significant changes. Most of the Roman or western rite liturgy was retained. The most substantive change in the mass was that the Eucharist was no longer considered a propitiatory sacrifice. This was reflected in Luther's *Latin Mass* (1523) and *German Mass* (1526) by greatly reducing the canon of the mass to remove all reference to sacrifice, but it was generally true of the 135 church orders adopted in various Lutheran territories until 1555. However, the Swedish Order of 1571 refers to the 'mass' as a sacrifice. Related to the concern that the mass not be viewed as a good work offered to God to win favour was the abolition of private masses and votive masses generally. While a Latin liturgy continued in communities where the language was understood, worship in the vernacular became more common and congregational singing of vernacular hymns was sung in both orders. In addition to changes in the mass, the daily prayer offices of matins and vespers, which had been mostly done in religious orders, were given new life as congregational prayer in the morning and evening.

Another significant change in corporate worship was recognition of two sacraments – baptism and Lord's Supper – rather than seven, although the other five continued in some form as sacred rites. In addition, preaching was based on gospel-centred interpretation of Scripture, rather than the traditional fourfold method using the literal, allegorical, moral, and eschatological meanings.[13]

The idea behind all this was that as long as the Word and sacraments are present and the gospel is served, the specific forms of worship used are *adiaphora*, not essential. Luther's thinking on such matters is clearly stated in his 1539 response to the chaplain of Electoral Brandenburg where the reformation was just being introduced and whose prince wanted to retain some traditional vestments and processions. Luther wrote:

> If your lord, the margrave and elector, will allow the gospel of Jesus Christ to be preached openly, clearly, and without admixture – and the two sacraments of baptism and the flesh and blood of Jesus Christ to be administered and given according to his institution, and will let the invocation of the saints fall away, so that they are not patrons, mediators, and intercessors, and the sacrament be not carried about in procession, and will let the daily masses and the vigils and requiems for the dead fall, and not have the water, salt, and herbs consecrated, and will sing pure responsories and songs in both Latin and German during the march or procession; then in God's Name, go along in the procession and carry a silver or golden cross, and a chasuble or an alb . . . For such matters, if free from abuses, take from or give to the gospel nothing; only they must not be thought necessary to salvation, and the conscience dare not be bound to them.[14]

Devotional Practices

There was a proliferation of devotional practices in the late Middle Ages. Medieval church scholar Richard Kieckhefer says devotional religion eludes precise definition, but he locates it roughly between liturgical exercises, that are public and official, and contemplative piety, that is basically private, unofficial, and unstructured. Devotional piety can be practised by individuals as well as by smaller or larger groups. Devotions can evolve from being unofficial and unstructured to being official and structured, as the Corpus Christi procession illustrates. According to Kieckhefer, medieval devotions are defined more by their objects than by their form, for they were usually directed to Mary, another saint, the suffering Jesus, or the consecrated host of the Eucharist.[15]

The rosary exemplifies the features of a devotion. The term 'rosary' referred to a cluster of prayers. Part of its remote origin seems to be the eleventh-century lay practice of reciting 150 Our Fathers as a substitute for saying the psalter, and many used a string of beads to count. As Marian piety increased in the twelfth century, the Hail Mary was added, and gradually rosaries dedicated to Mary developed. Dominicans promoted the devotion through lay associations, confraternities. Reciting this rosary was, and still is, a devotional practice done by individuals, but also by small or large groups.

Kieckhefer points out that there was also a strong penitential aspect to late medieval devotions, for there was often a close link between devotions and indulgences. Another underpinning for various devotions was the teaching of Purgatory as a state of purification from venial sins and temporal punishment for sin. Participation in certain devotional practices was encouraged by granting an indulgence which would reduce time in Purgatory.

Although Luther's objections to indulgences ignited the Reformation, his theology undercut many medieval devotions besides those specifically connected with indulgences. The Lutheran focus on both biblical authority and the gospel with its centre in justification by faith resulted in criticism of many late medieval devotional practices. For instance, while Mary and other saints are to be remembered and honoured as examples of God's grace at work, they should not be invoked in prayer. The gospel proclaims only Christ as Saviour, and Scripture lacks support for the practice. As Melanchthon says, 'Because neither a command, nor a promise, nor an example from Scripture about invoking saints can be brought forward, it follows that the conscience can find no certainty about such invocation.'[16] As a result, individual and corporate use of the rosary was discouraged. Because late medieval Eucharistic devotions were supported and spurred by the doctrine of transubstantiation officially proclaimed in 1215, these devotions were undercut by Lutheran rejection of that doctrine.

The devotional practices that Luther promoted were gospel-centred and practised by families and individuals. He stressed use of the Ten Commandments, the Creed, and the Lord's Prayer. Bible reading was also encouraged, and was made more possible by the invention of printing in the previous century. Singing of hymns and songs was also encouraged, and Lutherans rapidly produced a number of hymn-books. Images also played a role in devotional practice, because catechisms, hymn-books, and Luther's translation of the Bible were often illustrated.

Instruction

Spiritual practice among Lutherans was also affected by changes in instruction and institutional life. Catechesis or instruction has played a very important role in Christian practice since the very beginning. In the first three centuries when mostly adults were baptized, they were instructed in the Way (cf. Acts 18:25-6). From the fourth century when postbaptismal instruction became common, believers were required to know at least the Lord's Prayer and Apostles' Creed. The Ten Commandments were generally added to this in the thirteenth century. During the Middle Ages instruction of the laity took place mainly in sermons, but the advent of printing in the fifteenth century brought many catechisms for laity.

Instruction played a major role in spreading and then consolidating the Lutheran Reformation, and both preaching and catechisms were instrumental. From 1516 Luther preached regularly on the Ten Commandments, Apostles' Creed, and Lord's Prayer. In 1529 Luther published his *Large Catechism* and *Small Catechism*. The latter included his interpretation of the standard three texts as well as explanations of baptism, Eucharist, confession, morning and evening prayers, table grace, and a table of duties.

Luther's evangelical theology is evident not only in the words of the *Small Catechism*, but in its very structure. The medieval order of the standard three texts was Apostles' Creed, Lord's Prayer, and Ten Commandments – the Commandments instructing believers on how to act out their faith. Luther changes the order to Commandments, Creed, and Lord's Prayer. This reflects his understanding of the Commandments' primary function as showing people their sin. So, as Luther said, the law shows people their disease, the Creed tells them where to find the necessary medicine (God), and the Lord's Prayer teaches them how to obtain it.[17]

Institutional Life

The Lutheran reform movement also brought about some major institutional changes. One of these was the near abolition of monasticism in Lutheran territories. In the century prior to the Reformation, there had been considerable criticism of monastic practice and efforts at reform. Criticism intensified from humanists such as Erasmus shortly before Luther burst onto the scene. These earlier criticisms were both about moral abuses and, in Erasmus' case, about whether monastic life is truly better than lay life. Luther attacked abuses in monastic practice, such as imposing vows on young persons, but he also denied that the 'religious' life is more holy than life in the world. His most fundamental concern was that monasticism often encouraged people to win God's favour by their good works, so it conflicted with justification by faith. While Luther did not insist that men and women leave monastic life, he said one could rightly follow the life only if done freely and without works righteousness. Many left monastic life, although women resisted more than men. In Lutheran territories most monastic communities dissolved and their property was seized by secular rulers. Commonly rulers took a substantial portion of the property or income for their administration and converted the rest to charitable use such as schools and hospitals. However, in Scandinavia monasteries slowly declined, and in Germany a few convents persisted in Lutheran territories.[18]

The disappearance of monastic communities in most Lutheran territories was an institutional change with extensive impact on spiritual practice. Previously the many buildings and members of religious communities, cloistered and mendicant, were visible reminders of the monastic spiritual path. It was a viable option for people, and for women it offered a distinct sphere to exercise leadership and about the only other possibility than marriage. Indeed, the primary locus of much spiritual practice in western Christianity was a separated monastic community. While there has always been lay spirituality, a large share of scholarship on Roman Catholic spirituality still focuses on religious orders. As monasticism declined in Lutheran areas, service in the roles of secular life was accentuated and spiritual practices such as prayer now had to be carried out by nearly everyone amidst worldly responsibilities.

A second institutional change with enormous effect on spiritual practice was the change in ecclesiastical administrative and judicatory authority. Lutherans broke with the papacy and bishops in communion with the pope. When those who supported and opposed the Lutheran reform movement gathered at Augsburg in 1530, they all considered themselves part of one Church. They had much in common. They all recognized the authority of Scripture, the ancient creeds, and much else in church tradition, but Lutherans severely criticized the conduct of the papacy and many bishops. Lutherans continued for some time to seek a free church council, that is, one not under papal control, but it never happened. Even before Luther appeared, the papacy had resisted calls for reform and renewal, in part fearful of a resurgence of the conciliarist idea that a church council is superior to the pope. After Luther's bitter attacks on the papacy, any critique of Rome was suspected of heresy. So the reforms enacted in Roman Catholicism at the Council of Trent (1545–63), in diocesan life and in religious orders, were under close papal supervision.[19] Since Lutherans were separated from the Roman ecclesiastical authority, they were free to enact changes in practice according to their own authoritative sources of wisdom.

Administrative and judicatory authority in Lutheran churches varied somewhat, for each territory adopted its own church order that generally contained provisions not only on doctrine and worship, but also on administration of church affairs. Since only a few bishops in Germany supported evangelical reforms and they were forced to resign by Rome, German Lutheran church orders generally provided for superintendents. Lutheran churches in the Scandinavian countries had bishops, and apostolic succession was preserved in Sweden. Yet the theological principle was that all ministerial offices, including bishop, exist to serve the gospel. Since pope and bishops, in Luther's estimation, were not doing this, as early as 1520 he appealed to princes to lead in reforming the Church. Over time, though, the influence of the civil ruler over church affairs increased, and the prince, in effect, became the superior bishop. Yet, as we said earlier, throughout Europe in the sixteenth century civil rulers had extensive influence over religion in their jurisdiction. So the difference in recognized judicatory authorities, Roman Catholic, Lutheran, or Reformed, had tremendous influence on spiritual practice.[20]

5. ATTENTION TO THE WORD

Faith and spiritual practice are intimately related. So far we have dealt with three key Lutheran faith affirmations. First, while we humans are free to make choices in worldly matters, we do not have the power to turn ourselves toward God even in the smallest degree. Much medieval religious practice was based on the idea that if we just make an honest effort – 'do what is in us' – God will add grace to make us truly pleasing. Luther and the Lutheran Confessions reject this idea and assert bondage of the will in relation to God, the position held by Augustine. Second, humans become right with God by grace alone through faith alone in Jesus Christ. Salvation is entirely the fruit of God's grace that forgives sin and transforms the sinner to be more like Christ. Since transformation is always incomplete in this life, the secure ground of acceptance with God is divine forgiveness. These gifts of forgiveness and transformation are received through faith that clings to Christ. Third, the authoritative sources of wisdom to which the Lutheran tradition looks for guidance in faith and practice are in descending order of importance: Scripture, ancient creeds and the sixteenth-century Lutheran Confessions, and other church tradition. We began to see how these faith affirmations affected some aspects of Lutheran spiritual practice in corporate worship, devotional life, instruction, and institutional life. Now we turn to the core Lutheran spiritual practices of attending to Word and sacrament. We begin with attention to the Word.

In *The Freedom of a Christian*, Luther asks how a righteous, free, and pious Christian comes into existence. He answers,

It does not help the soul if the body is adorned with the sacred robes of priests or dwells in sacred places or is occupied with sacred duties or prays, fasts, abstains from certain kinds of food, or does any work that can be done by the body and in the body . . . One thing, and only one thing, is necessary for Christian life, righteousness, and freedom. That one thing is the most holy Word of God, the gospel of Christ . . .

Luther goes on to say, 'Faith alone is the saving and efficacious use of the Word of God . . .'[1] So what is vital for Christian existence is the Word of God received by faith.

'Word of God' is a complex metaphor for communication from God. In the Old Testament God creates by speaking and speaks through the prophets. In the New Testament the Word of God takes on additional meaning as the Christian message of salvation in Jesus Christ, who is the eternal Word become flesh. This Christian message of salvation is conveyed in the oral Word that testifies to Jesus Christ, in the written Word of Scripture, and in the visible Word of sacrament. Hence, Word of God has multiple meanings for Lutherans. Jesus Christ is the Word of God in the fullest sense. Yet most often Word of God refers to verbal forms of divine communication – oral and written – in distinction from sacraments with their physical signs, but at times it also bears the general meaning of communication from God and so sacraments can be called visible Word.

Since the Word of God in its various forms is communication from God, there is power in it, like the power of God's Word in creation. Through certain words or signs God speaks now to this person or group, and this divine communication makes things happen. Above all God's address elicits faith. God creates faith through the external means of words and sacramental signs that testify to Christ, the heart of God's saving truth. In contrast to some Reformation era leaders who spoke of unmediated revelations from God, Lutherans emphasized that Christian faith is not evoked apart from these external means of grace. Thus the fundamental Lutheran spiritual practices consist in attending to the means by which God creates and nourishes faith – Word and sacrament. While this had been and continues to be widespread Christian practice, Lutherans have given this catholic practice an evangelical interpretation. In this chapter we will examine some Lutheran practices of attending to the Word in verbal form.

A community's practices of attending to the Word always take place within that community's framework of interpreting the Christian message. Different interpretative frameworks are obvious already in the New Testament, for instance, when we compare the Gospel of John with the Gospel of Matthew. So also the Lutheran community tends to carry out its attention to the Word within a context that includes the previous core convictions as well as the dialectic of law and gospel.

Law and Gospel

Luther emphasized repeatedly that the Word of God comes as law and gospel, and that both are essential for the life of the Church. For Luther law is God's requirement, commandment, and judgement; gospel is God's promise, gift, and salvation. Law is most obviously expressed in commandments, gospel in the message of salvation in Christ. Both need to be proclaimed again and again.

On the one hand, Luther generally distinguished two uses or functions of the law. One is the civic or political function of the law. Here God provides order in society through the laws and expectations of governments, teachers, and parents. To observe such laws leads to civil righteousness, which is very useful for social cohesion, but does not bring right relation with God. The second and proper theological function of the law is to make people aware of their sin and need for salvation. So proclamation of the law in its theological function is necessary for repentance.

Several disputes took place among Lutherans over what is usually called the third use of the law, that is, whether the law should also serve as instruction and guide for Christians. Some

Lutherans thought this third use of the law would burden the conscience of Christians again with living up to the demands of the law and so lose an important element of Christian freedom. Although Luther did not formally distinguish a third use of the law, Melanchthon did, and with some cautions Article 6 of the *Formula of Concord* supported it.[2]

The gospel, on the other hand, announces God's gift of salvation, and faith is the appropriate response to the gospel. So, as we saw above, Luther says, 'One thing, and only one thing, is necessary for Christian life, righteousness, and freedom. That one thing is the most holy Word of God, the gospel of Christ . . . Faith alone is the saving and efficacious use of the Word of God.'

The distinction between law and gospel is a critical interpretative tool in Lutheran preaching, soul care, and spiritual practice. While both law and gospel are essential, it is also necessary to distinguish carefully between them. One reason this can be a subtle undertaking is that passages of Scripture usually cannot be designated simply as either law or gospel. For instance, the listing of the Ten Commandments in Exodus 20:3-17 is prefaced by a word of gospel, 'I am the Lord your God, who brought you out of the land of Egypt, out of the house of slavery.' The giving of God's commandments is grounded in God's prior gracious act of deliverance from slavery. On the other hand, the gospel-rich words of John 3:16 include reference to law in the possibility of perishing through failure to believe.

Distinguishing law and gospel is subtle also because it's not only a matter of interpreting Scripture, but also of interpreting the real-life situation being addressed. For example, if persons are already feeling as though God's heavy hand of judgement is on them in their suffering, then gospel should be stressed. But if a person or group is full of hubris, then priority should be given to law.

The distinction between law and gospel was vital not only for interpretation of Scripture in preaching and soul care, but also for observance of religious practices. Luther's persistent critique of a religion of 'good works' was aimed mainly at the idea that doing various religious acts would gain a person some advantage with God. What counted as 'good works' were not so much moral good deeds such as feeding the poor, but more commonly it was acts of piety such as venerating relics of a saint, saying so many prayers, and paying for masses to be said on someone's behalf. To approach God with this mindset, according to Luther, is to confuse law and gospel. Right relation with God is God's own gift (gospel), not the result of fulfilling some requirement (law).

Luther also criticized church leaders for not clearly distinguishing different kinds of law. He said they unnecessarily burdened people's consciences by confusing church rules about religious practice with God's law. For instance, a church rule about fasting on Friday was easily misunderstood by people as God's law. This confusion of church law with God's law was a form of spiritual bondage from which people should be set free. Consequently Luther was cautious about establishing new standard practices for all reformed churches, because the Christian life is a life of willing service to God and others – genuine freedom.

Operating with the distinction between law and gospel, Luther sought to make the Word of God more accessible to people. He did this through good translation of the Bible, a focus on preaching, changes in liturgy, and an emphasis on the Word in music. We shall discuss each of these in turn.

Translations of the Bible

One way to encourage attention to the Word was to make the Bible more accessible to people in their own language. At the beginning of the Reformation period the Latin Vulgate was the common Bible of western Christianity. Although there were numerous vernacular translations of the Latin Bible in existence, their use by heretical groups elicited efforts by authorities in some regions to restrict their publication. Martin Luther forged a new path in 1522 when he translated the New Testament from Greek into High German, and he went on to translate the Old Testament from Hebrew. He published the complete Bible with the Apocrypha in 1534. Luther himself knew Greek and Hebrew rather well, and he was helped in his ongoing work of revision by linguistic experts at the University of Wittenberg. Luther's great achievement in translation was to avoid stiff literalism and render the original languages in fresh contemporary German.[3]

In most other Lutheran territories outside of Germany the Bible was also quickly translated into the vernacular, although most of these versions relied heavily on Luther's German translation. For example, a translation into Danish was issued in 1524, another in 1529, and the whole Bible in 1543, but all were based upon the Latin Vulgate and Luther's German translation rather than on the original languages. In Sweden, though, the reformer Olaus Petri, assisted by Laurentius Andreae, based his 1526 translation of the New Testament on the Greek text as well as on the Latin translation and Luther's German version.

By Luther's death in 1546 over 430 editions of his translation of the Bible or selections from it had been published.[4] While vernacular translation of the Bible made the reading of Scripture more accessible for some in private use and more understandable in worship for the vast majority, who did not know Latin, it was many years before most ordinary people owned a Bible. Norwegian church historian Einar Molland says of Norway, 'As elsewhere, the Bible did not become a book for the common man before the age of Pietism, and in the strictest sense not before the 19th century. The cost of printing and the prevailing illiteracy were insurmountable obstacles against putting the Bible into the hands of the common people.'[5]

Another way to promote attention to Scripture was to make portions of the Bible available in translation. Luther did this in his *Personal Prayer Book* (1522). A practice common among Lutherans of later generations until today has been to use the Daily Texts, *Loesungen*, distributed from Herrnhut by the Moravians since 1731.

Preaching

'Revival in Church life has frequently been led by a revival in preaching and an insistence on the better education of the clergy.'[6] This was true in the twelfth and thirteenth centuries with Francis of Assisi and Dominic Guzman, and the religious orders they founded. It was true also of most sixteenth-century reform movements, including the Catholic reformation. Preaching also played a major role in the Lutheran reformation starting with Luther himself. A revival in preaching was much needed at the end of the Middle Ages. 'Though there was provision for scripture reading and a homily in vernacular languages, the lections often were omitted in favor of readings from the lives of the saints. In many parishes sermons were rarely heard, because local priests were too poorly trained to be capable of preaching.'[7] However, there were preaching missions held from time to time, and from this developed a vernacular service of the Word known as the Prone.[8]

Luther stressed preaching by elevating its significance and increasing its frequency. First, the significance of preaching was elevated, because Luther thought of it as the primary form of the living and present Word of God. The purpose of Christian preaching has differed in various times and situations. Duke Professor of Preaching Richard Lischer says, 'Of the many purposes for Christian preaching, the four dominant types are missionary preaching, instruction in the faith, liturgical preaching, and moral guidance.'[9] Whereas the thirteenth-century Franciscan Berthold of Regensburg, whose dramatic style made him probably the most popular preacher of the whole Middle Ages, called chiefly for moral reform, Luther stressed the call of the gospel.[10] For Luther the main purpose is kerygmatic or missionary preaching, and instruction in the faith is close behind. In the preaching situation God confronts listeners through law and gospel and calls them to repentance and faith. Luther says,

> It is not enough or in any sense Christian to preach the works, life, and words of Christ as historical facts . . . yet

this is the fashion among those who must today be regarded as our best preachers. Far less is it sufficient or Christian to say nothing at all about Christ and to teach instead the laws of men and the decrees of the fathers. Now there are not a few who preach Christ and read about him that they may move men's affections to sympathy with Christ, to anger against the Jews, and such childish and effeminate nonsense. Rather ought Christ to be preached to the end that faith in him may be established that he may not only be Christ, but be Christ for you and me, and that what is said of him and is denoted in his name may be effectual in us. Such faith is produced and preserved in us by preaching why Christ came, what he brought and bestowed, what benefit it is to accept him. This is done when that Christian liberty which he bestows is rightly taught . . .[11]

Second, Luther increased the frequency of preaching in Wittenberg. 'Since the preaching and teaching of God's Word is the most important part of divine service, we have arranged for sermons and lessons as follows: For the holy day or Sunday we retain the customary Epistles and Gospels and have three sermons.' At matins early in the morning the sermon was on the epistle lesson for the day, at the mass on the gospel lesson, and at vespers on the Old Testament chapter by chapter. 'This we think provides sufficient preaching and teaching for the lay people. He who desires more will find enough on other days.' Daily mass was suppressed in favour of daily preaching services: Monday and Tuesday mornings on the five parts of the catechism, Wednesday morning on the Gospel of Matthew, Thursday and Friday mornings on the Epistles and other parts of the New Testament, and Saturday afternoon on the Gospel of John. 'Thus enough lessons and sermons have been appointed to give the Word of God free course among us, not to mention the university lectures for scholars.'[12]

Since each Lutheran territory or country had its own church order with provisions for public worship, the pattern in

Luther's Wittenberg was not necessarily followed elsewhere. Furthermore, the severe lack of education among pastors could not be quickly overcome. In situations where the pastor was ill equipped to preach, Luther recommended that he read out a good sermon from among those published. None the less, in cities frequent preaching was common for many years. When Philip Spener wrote *Pia Desideria* in 1675 in Frankfurt am Main, he said, 'It may appear that the Word of God has sufficiently free course among us inasmuch as at various places (as in this city) there is daily or frequent preaching from the pulpit.'[13] During J.S. Bach's tenure as cantor (1723–50) in the Lutheran Orthodox city of Leipzig daily services with preaching were co-ordinated among the city's churches.[14] While today daily preaching services are uncommon except in Lutheran academic settings, preaching is still regarded as a very high pastoral responsibility, and care is taken to provide good education for those who are called to this public office.

The Word in Liturgy

Another way Luther made the Word more accessible was in the words and music of liturgy. As we have already seen, Luther initiated some profound changes in liturgical worship for ordinary lay people at the same time as he retained almost all the western rite liturgy. We can appreciate the change better against the background of late medieval worship. The highly respected British worship scholar and hymn-writer Brian Wren gives this imaginative reconstruction of the worship experience on Easter Sunday in northern Germany in 1451:

> Today . . . as for many years to come, Mass is celebrated in the sacred, time-honored way. The priest mumbles or whispers from his leather-bound, scribe-copied, illumi-nated Missal. The choir chants or sings from scribe-copied, leather-bound cantatories, and antiphonaries. The people neither read nor speak. On Friday they joined in the sorrowful songs of the passion play. Next week, they will

sing together on pilgrimage. At Sunday Mass, they are silent . . .

Mass begins. Procession, music, incense, vestments. Priest and choir have seats and stalls; ordinary people stand, pray silently, listen, and look. The Kyrie, Credo, Sanctus, Benedictus, and Agnus Dei, in olden times sung by the people, are beautifully elaborated by the choir. The priest stands, kneels, and genuflects at the high altar; the people watch from a safe distance. The bread and wine are holy; it is dangerous to get too near. Unworthy people shrink from the risk of touching holy ground. Receiving the wine at Communion has long been unthinkable. Receiving the bread is so terrifying that church authorities have to enforce yearly reception.

At Mass elsewhere in Europe, the people are intent and watchful, but silent. Germany has a different tradition. Today, as on other high days, a short song is sung by all. The choir leads off, accompanied by the organ, and the congregations sings, from memory, the popular Leise, 'Christ ist erstanden' . . .[15]

The mass was in Latin, which only the learned understood. The priest intoned some parts, and said others quietly beyond the hearing of the congregation. For the most part only the choir sang, because over several centuries the music had developed by stages from chanted melody to polyphony, where different musical lines interweave. The beautiful, awe-inspiring music was too difficult for untrained voices. Not that congregational singing disappeared altogether, for it was present sometimes in the mass and often in various devotional practices outside the mass. It was prominent in the missions of St Francis, and in Germany pilgrimage songs were popular.[16] The worship experience at mass for most ordinary folk was largely passive, and had its high point in seeing the consecrated elements.

Luther substantially changed the practice and experience of worship by making the Word more available to people in liturgy. He made changes in two stages. The first stage was to revise the Latin mass, which he wanted to continue among students and others who knew the language. In his revision of the Latin mass in 1523 Luther made the Word of the gospel more apparent by removing what he regarded as elements inconsistent with the gospel. He dropped portions of the offertory and canon that spoke of the Eucharist as a sacrifice, for he regarded that belief contrary to the gospel. Yet he did it in such a way that to those who did not know Latin, the change may have passed unnoticed. He retained the elevation of the bread and cup with the ringing of bells.

Luther's caution reflects the situation at the time. After he appeared before the emperor at the Diet of Worms in 1521, his prince kept him in hiding at the Wartburg for almost a year. During his absence, Andreas Karlstadt initiated radical changes in worship at Wittenberg that upset many people. Luther returned to restore order. So when he published his revision of the Latin mass in December, 1523, Luther wanted to avoid what he called 'frivolous faddism'.[17]

Luther made more extensive changes in the practice and experience of worship when he prepared a vernacular mass for the common people, *The German Mass and Order of Service* (1526). A number of German masses had already been prepared by others in the early 1520s, but Luther had aesthetic reservations about rushing the process. In 1524 he wrote,

> I would gladly have a German mass today. I am also occupied with it. But I would very much like it to have a true German character. For to translate the Latin text and retain the Latin tone or notes has my sanction, though it doesn't sound polished or well done. Both the text and notes, accent, melody, and manner of rendering ought to grow out of the true mother tongue and its inflection, otherwise all of it becomes an imitation, in the manner of apes.[18]

Luther wanted both good German verse and music that fit the rhythms of the language. For this he gained the assistance of two musicians in the service of the Elector of Saxony, Conrad Rupsch and Johann Walther. The results were German words and chant tones for priest and congregation as well as provision for German hymns and singing of the creed by the congregation.

Luther urged others not to make this order of service 'a rigid law to bind or entangle anyone's conscience, but use it in Christian liberty as long, when, where, and how you find it to be practical and useful.'[19] However, he believed Christian liberty in worship order should be exercised with care not to upset others needlessly, so he offered additional suggestions without insisting upon them.

> Here we retain the vestments, altar, and candles until they are used up or we are pleased to make a change. But we do not oppose anyone who would do otherwise. In the true mass, however, of real Christians, the altar should not remain where it is, and the priest should always face the people as Christ doubtlessly did in the Last Supper. But let that await its own time.[20]

The Word in Music

Another area in which Luther had a great effect on worship was by fostering attention to the Word in music, both in congregational singing and art music. Luther's very positive view of music contrasts with the attitudes of many Christian leaders toward music in worship. Most negative was Ulrich Zwingli, who banned music altogether from worship. Even though he was personally well trained in art music, Zwingli's interpretation of the Bible led him to believe that singing and instrumental music did not belong in congregational worship. Among those who permitted music in worship, ambivalence about the persuasive power of music has been common. Augustine appreciated the power of sung words to stir the heart to greater devotion than words not sung, yet he worried that this power of music might overshadow the message in the words.

Similarly John Calvin saw music as a gift from God, but was very concerned about the possibilities for corruption. In his view, worship should accord with the explicit witness of Scripture. Since the Bible says that Jesus and the apostles sang, but makes no mention of their using musical instruments, Calvin endorsed only the singing of psalms in unison without accompaniment. To meet Calvin's desire for weighty melodies appropriate to praising God, a professional musician, Louis Bourgeois, was commissioned to set the psalms to music. The outcome was the Genevan Psalter, with each of the 150 psalms translated into metered French and set to its own tune. Aside from occasional revisions, this remained the Reformed hymnal for many years to come; there was no room for adding additional hymns. Outside congregational worship many Reformed Christians sang the same psalm tunes either in harmony with instruments or in polyphonic settings by Bourgeois and others. For Calvin plain singing belonged in church, art music belonged outside of church.[21]

John Wesley also expressed ambivalence toward music. While encouraging worshippers to sing out, he cautioned, 'Attend strictly to the sense of what you sing, and see that your heart is not carried away with the sound, but offered to God continually.'[22] Like Augustine and Calvin, Wesley was worried that attention to the words would be overwhelmed by the music.

Luther's more positive view of music laid the foundation for both congregational singing and art music in worship. Luther saw music as an excellent gift of the Creator that is present in all creatures, for the air as well as all living things make sound and harmony. Yet the human voice surpasses them all with the variety of its music.

> Next to the Word of God, music deserves the highest praise. She is a mistress and governess of those human emotions – to pass over the animals – which as masters

govern men or more often overwhelm them. No greater
commendation than this can be found – at least not by us.
For whether you wish to comfort the sad, to terrify the
happy, to encourage the despairing, to humble the proud,
to calm the passionate, or to appease those full of hate . . .
what more effective means than music could you find?

Thus it was not without reason that the fathers and
prophets wanted nothing else to be associated as closely
with the Word of God as music . . . After all, the gift of
language combined with the gift of song was only given to
man to let him know that he should praise God with both
word and music, namely, by proclaiming [the Word of God]
through music and by providing sweet melodies with
words.[23]

Although Luther recognized that music could be perverted to
evil purposes, his primary emphasis is on the goodness of
music itself distinct from words. At the risk of scandalizing his
own Reformed tradition, Brian Wren endorses Luther's more
affirmative view of music. Wren says, 'It is inadequate to regard
the tunes we sing merely as a means of vocalizing their lyrics.'[24]
The music itself conveys another dimension of meaning. So in
a hymn when the meaning of the music and the meaning of the
words are not only compatible, but well matched, '"The music
dramatizes, explains, underlines, 'breathes life' into the words,
resulting in more meaning than the words themselves could
express" and a more powerful effect than text or music alone.'[25]
With appreciation of this meaning-making power of music,
Luther promoted proclamation of the Word of God with congregational hymns and art music in worship.

Erik Routley, a widely published authority on church music,
says hymnody as we know it now, started with Luther. It was
Luther 'who successfully propagated the idea that the communal singing of Christian songs could be an integral part of
public worship. People had plenty of religious songs before his
time; but not at the Mass, not at the centre of worship, and not
songs known all over Europe.'[26] Luther promoted congrega-

tional hymnody by writing hymns, encouraging others to do so, and supporting publication of worship music. Luther wrote thirty-six songs in all, twenty-three of them during 1523–4 as an incentive to others. He also supported the publication of hymns and collections of worship music. The first Protestant hymnal, the *Eight Song Book*, appeared in 1523–4 with four of its songs by Luther. Numerous hymnals and music collections were published within a few years. Various parts of the liturgy and catechism were set to chorale tunes. In 1545 at Luther's urging the first comprehensive collection of Latin and German hymns and chants used in the Lutheran liturgy was published.[27]

The Lutheran tradition of writing and arranging new hymn texts and tunes has continued down to the present. Among the best of many fine hymn-writers were Germans Philipp Nicolai (1556–1608, 'Wake, Awake, for Night Is Flying') and Paul Gerhardt (1607–76, 'O Lord, How Shall I Meet You'), Danes Thomas Kingo (1634–1703, 'On My Heart Imprint Your Image') and N.F.S. Grundtvig (1783–1872, 'Built on a Rock the Church Doth Stand'), Swede Johan Olaf Wallin (1779–1839, 'All Hail to You, O Blessed Morn'), and Norwegian Magnus Landstad (1802–80, 'I Know of a Sleep in Jesus' Name'). A flood of new hymns and songs pours out from a number of contemporary writers, and time will tell which works will last.

While a solid grounding in art music has often informed composition of Lutheran liturgy and congregational hymns, there has been greater scope for creativity in works for more accomplished musicians. This was already happening in 1524 which saw the publication of the *Spiritual Hymn Booklet* containing arrangements of thirty-seven hymns by Johann Walter, twenty-four of them composed by Luther, in three to five parts for choir. Such polyphonic settings were used by a choir alternating on the often lengthy hymns with the congregation singing in unison. The organ provided improvised prelude and interludes on the hymns, but did not accompany the singers until the seventeenth century.

Luther's practice of using art music in worship developed

further and continues yet today. In Lutheran territories of Germany it was customary for royal courts, towns, and cities to have a musical director or cantor to provide music for various occasions, including worship. The following description of the first half of the Christmas morning service in 1659 at the Church of St Nicholas in Berlin is given by Paul Gerhardt (1607–76), hymn-writer and deacon at this church whose long-time cantor was composer Johann Cruger (1598–1662).

> A group of schoolboys is at one side of the gallery and a choir of mixed voices at the other side. Below the pulpit we see a Collegium Musicum, a voluntary musical society composed of tradesmen and craftsmen, who perform on violins and wood-wind instruments, gathered around a small moveable organ. Then there is a male quartet, also a military band with trumpets, kettledrums and drums.
>
> After the organ prelude a chorale [Lutheran hymn] is sung . . . The entire liturgy is sung in Latin [the use of Latin or German varied from place to place] by the choirs and the schoolchildren. Next a college student, dressed as an angel with large white wings, sings from the pulpit an Old Testament prophecy, accompanied by the Collegium Musicum below.
>
> More chanting from the altar, and then the principal door of the church opens, and in comes a procession of girls, headed by the teacher, all dressed as angels. They proceed to the high altar, where the teacher sings the first verse of 'Vom Himmel hoch' and the second verse is sung by the girls in two-part counterpoint. The third verse is taken by the organ and the choir in the gallery as a beautiful five-part motet. While the procession has been marching down the aisle, one of the ministers chants a 'Gloria' answered by the electoral court and field trumpeters with fanfares and drumrolls.[28]

In this service young and old and people of different social classes – from tradesmen and craftsmen to the royal family – are engaged in worshipping God with fine music.

At the top of the long list of Lutheran composers of art music for worship stand Michael Praetorius (1571–1621), Heinrich Schutz (1585–1672), perhaps the greatest composer of the seventeenth century, and J.S. Bach (1685–1750), the greatest of the eighteenth century. Borrowing musical forms from composers of opera and Roman Catholic liturgical works, Lutheran composers in the seventeenth and eighteenth centuries wrote thousands of musical interpretations of Scripture texts – choral motets and more complex cantatas with solo voices. For example, between the reading of a Gospel text and the sermon on it might come a choral interpretation of that text. Another option was to sing the motet during the ministration of Holy Communion. In these ways the service might achieve a deep unity of word and music. Lutheran composers also wrote musical interpretations of Gospel accounts of Christ's passion for Holy Week with roles for several characters as well as the congregation. Some of these, such as the most famous St John Passion and St Matthew Passion of J.S. Bach, reached the complexity and length of the oratorio, which was meant for use outside a normal worship service.

This tradition of religious art music is still alive among Lutherans. During the twentieth century Germany produced a substantial number of exceptional church music composers including Hugo Distler (1908–42). In the United States many Lutheran colleges have had outstanding music faculties and excellent choirs that have fostered the composition and singing of sacred art music both for worship and the concert hall. Americans Richard Hillert, Paul Bouman, and Carl Schalk, inspired by the German renewal, have been especially active in composing and arranging fine religious music.

Culture can be both a pathway and an obstacle for proclaiming the Word of God in music. While the Lutheran emphasis on religious art music has been a powerful inspiration for many, it also has the potential for losing contact with ordinary people. Music historian Friedrich Blume suggests that Lutheran concentration on Latin art music in the post-reformation era created a gap between the educated and uneducated that opened the door to the spread of the Reformed church in Germany. Frank Senn comments, 'Lutheranism's openness to and promotion of the highest expressions of culture has sometimes proven to be more than can be profitably absorbed by the ordinary members of the community of faith.'[29] In the United States Lutheran translator and writer of hymn texts Gracia Grindal argues that those who chose the liturgical music and hymns in the 1978 *Lutheran Book of Worship* fostered such a gap, and she encourages more use of folk melodies and songs that touch the heart, such as those of Swede Carolina Sandell-Berg (1832–1903, 'Thy Holy Wings'). Among contemporary writers who have created more lyrical music, some of which will likely endure, are Americans John Ylvisaker ('I was there to hear you borning cry') and Marty Haugen ('Healer of our every ill' and several liturgies). In Germany some cantors are using more popular musical forms, as I found on a Sunday morning in February 1997 at the Stiftskirche in Wunsdorf near Hannover. After a reading of the gospel text on the story of Jairus' daughter, we heard a cantata on the text composed by the congregation's cantor. While several youth played recorders and the cantor played electronic keyboard, other youth and he sang parts in the biblical story. The music was reminiscent of Andrew Lloyd Webber's musical *Joseph and the Amazing Technicolor Dreamcoat*. The church was full, and congregational singing of traditional hymns was strong.

Lutherans whose culture is different from the high culture of the West have taken up the work of singing the Lord's song in their own musical idioms. While churches in Africa, Asia, and Latin America generally continue to sing some hymns brought from Europe or North American by immigrants or missionaries, they are adding tunes and texts from their own culture. In India some congregations sing biblical stories with traditional folk melodies, while others adapt traditional dances and chants with Christian content. In Tanzania local people sometimes use African melodies and rhythms to compose a new song to fit a biblical text.[30] It is customary for

Tanzanian Lutheran choirs participating in choir contests to sing both hymns brought by missionaries and African hymns. The musical witness of these Lutherans is beginning to enrich the songs used by European and North American Lutherans. *With One Voice* (1995) and the *Renewing Worship Songbook* (2003) are American supplemental worship resources that include songs from many cultures.

This process of cultural adaptation has also been happening among Afro-Americans and Latin Americans in the United States. For example, in a Sunday service I attended in 1996 at Bethany Lutheran Church, an Afro-American congregation in Chicago, a liturgy from the *Lutheran Book of Worship* was sung upbeat and with syncopation. The choir processed with rhythmic step, and the choir anthem was a black gospel number sung with such power and emotion by the choir and soloist that by the end they (and most of the congregation) had tears in their eyes. The congregation sang from the *Lutheran Book of Worship* Luther's original syncopated version of 'A mighty fortress is our God' and the standard Protestant hymn 'The church's one foundation', and then from a printed sheet the gospel song 'Lead me, guide me'. Now this church and others can use liturgies, hymns, and songs from *This Far by Faith: An African American Resource for Worship* (1999).[31]

Amid ongoing debates about what music is appropriate for worship, Lutherans are extremely blessed to have such a rich heritage of attending to the Word in music, a heritage that is still very much alive. Making the Word accessible has been a strong emphasis ever since Luther. In this chapter we have examined how attention to the Word has been fostered not only through music but also through good translations of the Bible, strong preaching, and gospel-centred liturgy. In the next chapter we will look at ways in which Lutherans have encouraged attention to the Word through prayer and devotional literature.

6. PRAYER AND DEVOTIONAL LITERATURE

Because Lutherans have taught that Christian faith lives from the Word of God in words and sacrament, their core spiritual practices include ways of attending to the Word. In chapter five we have already examined how this was done through Bible translations, preaching, liturgy, and music. Two other prominent ways that Lutherans have promoted attention to the Word are prayer and devotional literature, for they have regarded both practices as properly centred on the Word.

Luther's Understanding of Prayer

Luther's understanding of prayer is articulated in three works, *An Exposition of the Lord's Prayer for Simple Laymen* (1519), *Large Catechism* (1529), and *A Simple Way to Pray* (1535), a treatise he wrote in response to his barber's request for help in this practice. Luther's conception of prayer can be summarized in four points. First, genuine prayer is from the heart, the centre of the human soul. Luther stresses this in part because he thought in his day among the laity, priests, and members of religious orders there was a lot of sham prayer performed only by the mouth. He says, 'Spiritual and sincere prayer reflects the heart's innermost desires, its sighing and yearning.' Sham prayer makes hypocrites, true prayer makes saints.[1]

Second, genuine prayer occupies one's attention. This too is partly directed against mere external prayer in which the mouth babbles and the mind wanders to other thoughts. 'But, praise God, it is now clear to me that a person who forgets what he has said has not prayed well. In a good prayer one fully remembers every word and thought from the beginning to the end of the prayer.'[2]

Third, God's Word encourages and warms our heart to approach God with our deepest desires. It does this in several ways. The most basic way is that God addresses us in and through the Word, calling us to pray, and this divine communication requires our response. God's Word even specifically commands us to pray, so any doubts we may have about the value of prayer or being worthy to pray may be overcome. God's command counters the human heart's tendency to flee from God. Another way is that God's Word contains some powerful promises that God hears and answers prayer. 'Such promises certainly ought to awaken and kindle in our hearts a longing and love for prayer.'[3] Yet another way God's Word encourages the human heart is by giving us the very words to pray – the Lord's Prayer. Whereas some might regard this as a prayer just for beginners, Luther regards it as the highest and truest form of prayer. At the age of fifty-two Luther wrote, 'To this day I suckle at the Lord's Prayer like a child, and as an old man eat and drink from it and never get my fill. It is the very best prayer, even better than the psalter, which is so very dear to me. It is surely evident that a real master composed and taught it.'[4]

Fourth, once the heart is warmed to prayer, one is not bound to a certain formula or to repetition of specific words. What counts are the thoughts. After explaining to Peter the barber how he interprets the petitions of the Lord's Prayer, Luther says:

> You should also know that I do not want you to recite all these words in your prayer. That would make it nothing but idle chatter and prattle, read word for word out of a book as were the rosaries by the laity and the prayers of the priests and monks. Rather do I want your heart to be stirred and guided concerning the thoughts which ought to be comprehended in the Lord's Prayer. These thoughts

may be expressed, if your heart is rightly warmed and inclined toward prayer, in many different ways and with more words or fewer...It may happen occasionally that I may get lost among so many ideas in one petition that I forego the other six. If such an abundance of good thoughts comes to us we ought to disregard the other petitions, make room for such thoughts, listen in silence, and under no circumstances obstruct them. The Holy Spirit himself preaches here, and one word of his sermon is far better than a thousand of our prayers.[5]

When we step back and look at Luther's understanding of prayer, we see that it is thoroughly dialogical. Throughout, prayer is a personal meeting with God, an I-Thou relationship. In this respect his view of prayer is fundamentally moulded by the Lord's Prayer and the Psalms. Because prayer is understood as an I-Thou relationship, the human partner is fully engaged both in heart and mind. The yearnings, joys, and sorrows of the heart are expressed, and one's attention is held. In the moments of an I-Thou encounter, one's mind does not wander off.

A familiar example of an I-Thou relationship between people is a heart-to-heart talk with another person. We know from experience how precious such a talk is, and how difficult it is to come by. All sorts of internal and external barriers and distractions arise. When we are not able to produce at will I-Thou experiences with one another, it is not surprising that we are unable to create them with God.

Luther believes it is God who takes the initiative in establishing these I-Thou moments by warming our heart and capturing our attention through the Word. For Luther the human role in approaching prayer is to turn to the Word of God, as it is expressed especially but not exclusively in the words of Scripture. So Luther describes his personal practice this way:

First, when I feel that I have become cool and joyless in prayer because of other tasks or thoughts (for the flesh and the devil always impede and obstruct prayer), I take my little psalter, hurry to my room, or, if it be the day and hour for it, to the church where a congregation is assembled and, as time permits, I say quietly to myself and word-for-word the Ten Commandments, the Creed, and, if I have time, some words of Christ or of Paul, or some psalms, just as a child might do.[6]

The purpose of this recitation or reading is to warm the heart for prayer.

Having warmed the heart through initial recitation of the Ten Commandments, the Apostles' Creed, and perhaps some other portions of Scripture, Luther's own practice was to recite the Lord's Prayer and then meditate slowly on one or more portions of it. After that, if he had time, he would meditate on the Ten Commandments by reflecting on each one from four angles – as instruction, thanksgiving, confession, and petition. If time and inclination allowed, he would then do the same with the Apostles' Creed. Again and again he used the Word to warm the heart for prayer and free himself from distractions.[7] In commenting on the use of the Ten Commandments in this way, Luther says one may not need to repeat many words: 'It is enough to consider one section or half a section which kindles a fire in the heart.'[8]

Luther's practice may seem boring, because it's so repetitive. Meditating on the same relatively few words day after day, year after year. Especially to focus on the Lord's Prayer, which is so short and simple. It would be different working with the whole Bible, because it's a huge collection of writings with ample variety. Of course, Luther knew the Bible extremely well, because as a professor of the whole Bible he lectured regularly on biblical books, he translated the entire Bible into German, and as a part-time pastor he preached on many texts. So all that biblical knowledge is there for him. Yet in his daily prayers he concentrates on three short catechetical texts. In part, this is probably just a matter of personal history and preference; this is what worked for him. But the underlying principle is that Luther believed the human heart needs to be trained and shaped for prayer by God's Word. We should not simply rely upon the natural desires of our heart as the springboard for prayer. The heart needs to have its desires reshaped. So returning again and again to the apparently simple Lord's Prayer is one way to teach the heart to desire what Jesus said we should seek.

According to Finnish Luther scholar Simo Peura, Luther's underlying conviction is that God works in and through the scriptural words to convey not only the meaning, but also the reality of Christ's life. *Theosis,* divinization, takes place through Christ present in the believer; the believer participates in Christ. Peura says,

> According to Luther, all words of Christ and all words which speak about Christ, are sacramental words. This is to say, that these words are sacramental signs which do not only refer to certain things they are speaking about, but are the means through which God offers us the reality itself, i.e. Christ and his spiritual gifts.

The Word warms and shapes the heart, because through the Holy Spirit the scriptural words have power to enlighten and transform human life.[9]

Although Luther severely criticized monastic prayers, Martin Nicol has shown that Luther also learned from meditation practices customary in his own Augustinian order.[10] Luther's own understanding of prayer has much in common with the fundamental conception of western monastic prayer through the eleventh century as delineated by the Benedictine scholar Jean Leclercq. Monastic prayer involved *lectio, meditatio,* and *oratio. Oratio,* speaking to God, was the goal; it was supposed to be pure (without distractions), and consequently had to be brief and frequent. What gave rise to *oratio* was frequent *lectio*, reading, commonly out loud, and meditation. Leclercq says, 'Meditation was exercised without constraint; it sufficed for it to be fostered by reading. Attention was aroused, stimulated by the text, and when it disappeared, this was the sign that it was time to resume reading in order to rekindle reflection.'[11] Luther's understanding of prayer as an I-Thou encounter grounded on God's Word agrees with this. The major difference is that whereas monastics withdrew from society and organized their life toward the goal of unceasing prayer, Luther counsels people living in the everyday world to make prayer the first and last business of the day.

How does Luther's understanding of prayer compare to that of those commonly designated Christian mystics? Here we may recall Bernard McGinn's distinction between mystical elements and explicit mysticism that we introduced in chapter three. Mystical elements are present in Christianity from the beginning: they are evident in Paul's 'in Christ' formula and 'It is not I who live, but Christ who lives in me', and in John's vine and branches motif. Explicit mysticism first appeared, says McGinn, when Origen's theory of mysticism received institutional embodiment in monasticism. While the goal of explicit or proper mysticism is an encounter that is often called 'union with God', McGinn says there have been several, maybe even many, understandings of this union down through the centuries. Hence he thinks it is best to interpret union with God broadly as some experience of the immediate or direct presence of God. Such immediate consciousness of God may happen through the usual practices of prayer, sacraments, and other rituals, but it need not. Explicit or proper mysticism is a whole way of life that is concerned with preparing for and responding to such immediate experiences.[12] A common theoretical component of this way of life has been distinction between several stages of the spiritual life, as with Origen and Dionysius.

While Luther shares with representatives of explicit mysticism an emphasis on training by frequent attention to the Word of God, he differs from most representatives of mysticism proper in several respects. First, Luther's conception of prayer does not put an emphasis on ecstatic experiences of God's presence. We can distinguish ecstatic experiences of God from more ordinary encounters, rather like a married couple would distinguish ecstatic moments in their life together from more usual I-Thou moments of intimacy. Christians generally would have some experiences of intimacy with God, experiences of God's presence. Those engaged in a contemplative or mystical way of life hold up as models those who have both ecstatic experiences and more ordinary experiences of God's presence. Ecstatic experiences of divine presence – what McGinn calls immediate or direct experience – tend to spill over into ordinary life and foster more low-key experiences of God's presence. Explicit mysticism has a theory and practice intended to nurture ecstatic experiences of divine presence. Although Luther's conception of prayer need not exclude ecstatic experiences of God, what he emphasizes is the ordinary I-Thou encounter with God.

Related to this is the second point. Unlike those who join a religious order with a contemplative orientation, Luther does not organize all of life around preparing for experiences of immediate consciousness of God, but stresses engagement in ordinary daily life. Third, Luther also does not distinguish stages of spiritual progress, such as purgation, illumination, and union. Fourth, Luther differs from strongly apophatic mystics who talk about the highest prayer experience as imageless, wordless union with God in which the cognitive distinction between self and other that normally structures human experience is temporarily surpassed although the ontological distinction remains.[13] Luther is not alone in this last respect, for St Teresa of Avila, the great Spanish cataphatic mystic a generation after Luther, also had reservations about it.[14] While Luther's dialogical conception of prayer has an important place for profound intimacy with God and union with Christ, the experiential distinction between the human self and the divine other always remains. So there are some mystical elements present in Luther's understanding of prayer, but they do not constitute explicit mysticism.

To summarize, Luther understands prayer as an I-Thou encounter with God in which the heart becomes engaged through attention to the Word of God.

Later Lutheran Conceptions of Prayer

The great Lutheran Orthodox theologian Johann Gerhard has very much the same understanding as Luther. In his *Sacred Meditations* (1606), following in the I-Thou tradition, Gerhard speaks of prayer as 'spiritual conversation between God and the devout soul'. He goes on to say that God-pleasing prayer is ardent and wise, for such prayer comes from the heart and a faith guided by Scripture. 'Faith, however, hath due regard to the Divine Word. What God promises absolutely in His Word, that thou mayest pray for absolutely; what He promises conditionally, as, for example, temporal blessings, those likewise thou shouldst ask for conditionally; what He has in no way promised thou shouldst in no way pray for.'[15] So while true prayer is heartfelt, the heart needs to be guided by the Word.

Johann Arndt, one-time pastor to the young Gerhard, also speaks of prayer as conversation with God and 'intercourse of the believing heart with God', but he introduces some ideas from explicit mysticism. Arndt distinguishes three forms and levels of prayer – oral, internal, and supernatural. As with Luther the external exercise of oral prayer has the function of elevating the heart to God and so leads to internal prayer or meditation, but he adds that this mental prayer gradually leads to supernatural prayer. Arndt quotes from the mystic Johann Tauler (1300–61) to describe supernatural prayer as 'a true union with God by faith; when our created spirit dissolves, as it were, and sinks away in the uncreated Spirit of God'. Arndt interprets this in I-Thou terms, for he says in supernatural prayer the soul 'can think of nothing else but of God only'. In this state the tongue ceases and other thoughts are experienced as intrusions. What the soul experiences here is beyond description.[16] These three levels of prayer correspond to the Dionysian three stages of spiritual life – purgation/repentance, illumination, and union with God.[17] Like Luther Arndt understands prayer as communion with God that at times becomes very intimate, but his conception of prayer reflects his greater theological emphasis on transforming grace or sanctification. He borrows a three-level view of prayer and the Christian life from mystical writers to express the idea of progress in sanctification. Arndt defends his use of such authors against those Lutheran theologians who saw this as contradictory to Lutheran doctrine on sin and justification, 'It is true that I have quoted, especially in the Frankfurt edition, some earlier writers, such as [Johann] Tauler, [Thomas] a Kempis, and others, who may seem to ascribe more than is due to human ability and works; but my whole book strives against such [an error].'[18] For Arndt new life is possible only by keeping the eye on Jesus Christ, and this requires attention to the Word.

Arndt, like Luther, stresses that true prayer comes from a heart shaped by the Word. The Pietist Spener follows him in this, but since, even more than Arndt, he lived in an age dominated by Orthodox theology, in his thinking head and heart are played off against each other. So, instead of scholastic theology which is satisfied with mere knowledge, he recommends the practical theology of mystical writers such as Tauler, Thomas à Kempis, Gerson, *The German Theology*, and similar works, because they stress 'practical purification, illumination, and union with God'. He admits that such works have some features inconsistent with Lutheran doctrine, for he says they contain some 'papal filth' and Platonic concepts. Nevertheless, they 'move and grasp the heart'.[19] In addition to Word, sacraments, and suffering as means to bring about true prayer, Spener encourages free prayer out of one's own heart rather than only using written or memorized prayers. The use of free prayer in corporate worship as well as private prayer often distinguished Pietists from other Lutherans.[20]

Over time Lutheran Pietism came to share more characteristics with pietistic movements that stressed a distinct conversion experience. We saw in chapter one that August Hermann Francke, having had such a conversion, thought it was the usual way God dealt with people, although not the only way. Within revivalistic Evangelicalism a common expression for conversion has been 'letting Jesus into your heart', and the same image also shaped the conception of heartfelt prayer among many pietistic Lutherans. For instance, Ole Hallesby (1879–1961), theology professor at Norway's Menighetsfakultetet, or Free Faculty, in his book *Prayer*, defines prayer, 'To pray is to let Jesus come into our hearts.'[21] This book was translated into Swedish, Danish, Finnish, and English, and sold widely among Lutherans until the latter part of the twentieth century. There are present in Hallesby many of Luther's individual notes on prayer such as praying from the heart in need, with faith in Christ, and with eyes on the Bible, yet the tune has been somewhat altered.

Dietrich Bonhoeffer's understanding of prayer is a solid return to Luther's conception. His guiding principle, as for Luther, is that prayer needs to be shaped by the Word of God. By this principle Bonhoeffer organized life in the small illegal seminary at Finkenwald from 1935 to 1937 to provide for communal and private prayer under the Word. Like the disciples we all need to ask, 'Lord, teach us to pray', and Jesus Christ teaches us especially through the Lord's Prayer and the Psalter. Like Luther Bonhoeffer says the Lord's Prayer includes everything that ought to be in a prayer, and the Psalms and Lord's Prayer mutually interpret each other. So he calls the Psalter 'the great school of prayer'. It teaches us to pray on the basis of divine promises, what we should pray including the calls for vengeance and claims of innocence, and always to pray as a community. Even the Psalter's repetitions are part of this teaching. Bonhoeffer says, 'Is this not an indication that prayer is not a matter of pouring out the human heart once and for all in need or joy, but of an unbroken, constant learning, accepting, and impressing upon the mind of God's will in Jesus Christ?'[22]

Bonhoeffer reaffirmed these ideas in his book on the psalms, *The Prayerbook of the Bible,* written in 1940. At a time when the so-called Christians in Nazi Germany were trying to cast off from Christianity Jewish elements such as the Psalter, Bonhoeffer stresses again that we need to learn from Jesus how to pray.

'To learn to pray' sounds contradictory to us. Either the heart is so overflowing that it begins to pray by itself, we say, or it will never learn to pray. But this is a dangerous error, which is certainly very widespread among Christians today, to imagine that it is natural for the heart to pray. We then confuse wishing, hoping, sighing, lamenting, rejoicing – all of which the heart can certainly do on its own – with praying. But in doing so we confuse earth and heaven, human beings and God. Praying certainly does not mean simply pouring out one's heart. It means, rather, finding the way to and speaking with God, whether the heart is full or empty. No one can do that on one's own. For that one needs Jesus Christ.[23]

Jesus teaches prayer not only through the Lord's Prayer but also through the Psalms, which he makes God's Word by using them as his own prayers. So Bonhoeffer articulates a principle basic for Luther and Gerhard, and shared in the main by Arndt and Spener: we need to learn to pray by having the Word of God shape our prayer. Consequently it has been common for Lutherans to encourage ways to pray with the Bible and biblically related materials. Praying with the Bible was made more accessible through good vernacular translations of the Bible about which we spoke in the last chapter. Another avenue for the Word to shape prayer is Bible-centred devotional literature, and Lutherans have created a large body of it.

Devotional Literature

Lutheran leaders of every era promoted devotional literature in keeping with their view of the Christian life. Luther was concerned to replace works-oriented writings with devotional works more consistent with Lutheran doctrine. With their shift toward greater emphasis on sanctification, Arndt and the Pietists drew more extensively from medieval and Puritan sources. A move toward moralism in devotional writing during the period of Enlightenment influence in the eighteenth century was followed during the early nineteenth-century awakening by a strong resurgence of interest in classic Lutheran devotional writings. The works of Luther and seventeenth-century authors as well as works by contemporary Neo-Lutherans such as Claus Harms and Wilhelm Loehe were in demand.

Devotional writings constitute a literary genre with many subgenres. These subgenres can be exhibited at various levels: most are rather pedestrian literary productions intended for the ordinary run of people, yet some are conceptually challenging writings intended for the intellectual elite and a few are literary works of high quality that appeal to a broad audience. We will consider six subgenres used widely among Lutherans.[24]

1. *Prayer books*. This is not a sharply defined category, for prayer books range from materials for meditation to collections of written prayers. Because the collections popular when Luther appeared on the scene, issued by printers apart from church control, were filled with exaggerated claims and promises of indulgences, he believed reform must also take place in this arena. So in 1522 he published his *Betbuchlein (Personal Prayer Book)* as an alternative. The consistent core of this book, whose content varied through different editions, was Luther's explanations of four texts which even illiterate people were expected to know – the Ten Commandments, Apostles' Creed, Lord's Prayer, and Hail Mary – so literate and illiterate could pray together. Although the words of the Creed were not from the Bible, Luther regarded its content as biblical. Very soon he added eight psalms, his German translation of Paul's Epistle to Titus, and fifty pictures of biblical stories. After his *Small Catechism* with its explanations of the three basic texts appeared in 1529, it tended to replace this prayer book.[25] With both books Luther encourages others to pray in a manner similar to his own pattern as described in his advice to Peter the barber, namely, meditating on the Commandments, Creed, and Lord's Prayer.

Although it does not appear that Luther's exact way of meditating on the three catechetical texts endured widely among Lutherans, his catechism continued to shape Lutheran piety. For example, the Danish theologian and historian Erik Pontoppidan (1698–1764), who was Bishop of Bergen, Norway, for six years, published a Pietist explanation of Luther's *Small Catechism* that had 759 questions and answers. It became Denmark's official catechism and was used in the public schools. When the layman Hans Nielsen Hauge (1771–1824) spearheaded a Pietist revival in Norway, he preached and taught with Luther's *Small Catechism* and Pontoppidan's explanation.[26]

Another kind of prayer book had written prayers for different occasions. Two popular collections of written prayers were Peter Treuer's *Betgloecklein*, which went through eight editions between 1579 and 1710, and Johann Friedrich Starck's *Das Taegliche Handbuch in Guten und Boesen Tagen* (1727), a daily handbook for good and bad days, which was used by many immigrants in America.

2. *Sermon books.* Down through the centuries Lutherans have published sermons which have been found especially successful in fostering prayer and guiding believers in difficult situations. The practice began with Luther, many of whose sermons were printed individually and in collections. For example, he added four of his sermons to the 1529 edition of his *Personal Prayer Book.* In many of his edifying sermons Luther used the format of dividing the exposition into brief numbered sections.[27] Some of Johann Arndt's sermons were also published throughout the seventeenth century and, as mentioned previously, Philip Spener's *Pia Desideria* was, in fact, written in 1675 as the preface to a new edition of Arndt's sermons. Sermons of Spener and Francke were also published. One of Christian Scriver's popular books was a five-volume set of weekday sermons under the title *Seelenschatz*, which was published between 1675 and 1692 and also translated into Danish, Finnish, Norwegian, and Swedish. One of the ways in which Norwegian Hans Nielsen Hauge spread his

message was by publishing a 900-page book of his sermons in 1800. Sermon books such as these were often used by Lutheran immigrants to North America when a pastor was not available.

3. *Books of meditations.* In 1519 Luther published a short piece entitled 'A Meditation on Christ's Passion' that was delivered as a sermon. The most popular collection of meditations was *True Christianity* in which Johann Arndt writes each chapter as a meditation on a verse or two of Scripture that he selects according to his overall purpose. Most chapters could be read in 5–15 minutes and are subdivided into paragraphs, so the material is presented in small pieces for prayerful rumination.

Another popular book of this type was *Sacred Meditations* (1606), a collection of short sermonic reflections by Johann Gerhard on co-ordinated themes of his choosing. Heinrich Mueller developed a number of sermons into lively meditations entitled *Spiritual Hours of Refreshment* (1664). Maybe most innovative was Christian Scriver's *Gotthold's Occasional Devotions* (1663), which consists of 400 meditations about one page long by a character named Gotthold who reflects on things he encounters. For instance, when Gotthold observes some sailors pulling a boat upstream on a river with ropes, he says, 'Here...I have a representation of my own voyage to heaven. The world is the powerful current which pulls many along with it into the sea of perdition. I, with my little ship, must struggle against this current because I have been commanded not to be conformed to the world, nor to love either it or its lusts. (Rom. 12:2; I John 2:15)'[28]

In works such as these the Word of God was being interpreted by the writer in small units that were very well suited to meditation. Most chapters were brief enough to be easily read in a few minutes, had a down-to-earth appeal to life like a good sermon, and often could easily be broken into yet smaller units for sharply focused reflection. Nicholas Hope says these and similar writings of the time constituted a 'devotional canon' that shaped the practice of piety among

Lutherans for several centuries.[29] However, in twentieth-century America meditation books were gradually replaced in most pious homes by small quarterly booklets of daily meditations such as *Portals of Prayer*. For each day of the year there is a page with a Scripture passage, brief meditation, and written prayer. Since these booklets continually change authors and content and their extreme brevity mirrors the fast-paced character of contemporary life, they do not have the enduring influence of more substantial meditation books.

4. *Hymn-books*. There is a long history of hymnic poetry being used in prayer, for the Psalms have been a staple of Jewish and Christian prayer for many centuries. The revival of congregational hymn-singing led by Luther and others created new material that could also be used in personal and small-group devotional practice. Lutheran hymn-books often contained written prayers for many occasions as well as Scripture readings for the church year, so they were useful for corporate worship and private devotions. Since hymns have a way of lodging in the heart and memory, it was common for Lutheran homes to own a hymn-book and use it devotionally. Lutheran immigrants to the US and Canada frequently included one among the very few books they took with them. Gustav Neumann says of these immigrants using hymns in the language of their youth and homeland, 'The hymns in the book were not so much sung as prayed. Stanzas from the hymns were memorized from earliest childhood and remained a basic staple of personal emotional expression.'[30] Because Lutheran immigrants often were in situations with an itinerant pastor, they managed worship most of the time on their own. One woman recalls the days without a pastor, '[We] would all dress in our Sunday clothes and father would lead the devotion. First we would sing hymns, then he would read prayers from the hymnbook, and then he had a book of long sermons by "Johan [sic] Arndt" which he would read very distinctly. This devotion would last for two hours.'[31]

The devotional use of hymns is still alive today among some Lutherans. I recall a 1997 meeting with three Tanzanian

Lutherans about their healing ministry; our meeting con-
cluded with spontaneous prayer and singing by memory
several stanzas of a Swahili hymn. Also in Decorah, Iowa
where I live, when a ninety-year-old woman's failing sight
made it impossible for her to read her old Lutheran hymnal
for personal devotions, she asked to have the words of her
favourite hymns recorded.

5. *Reprints, translations, and selections of non-Lutheran
devotional writings.* Medieval and contemporary Catholic
devotional writings were used, sometimes without attribution. Luther was the first to introduce this practice when in
1516 he had printed the fourteenth-century *Theologia
Germanica (The German Theology)* from a manuscript in
German that he found and in 1518 published a larger version
of it based upon another, fuller manuscript. He says in his
preface to the later edition, 'Next to the Bible and Saint
Augustine no other book has come to my attention from which
I have learned – and desire to learn – more concerning God,
Christ, man, and what all things are.'[32] Several times Johann
Arndt reprinted *The German Theology* as well as a German
translation of *The Imitation of Christ* by Thomas à Kempis. In
addition, in his *True Christianity* Arndt borrowed freely from
writings of Johann Tauler, whom he cited, but also without
attribution from the thirteenth-century mystic Angela of
Foligno and seventeenth-century Jesuit Valentine Weigel.[33] In
his very popular compilation of prayers, *Betgloeklein*, Peter
Treuer borrowed from contemporary Catholic authors without
acknowledging his sources. Among his proposals for improv-
ing church life in *Pia Desideria* Philip Spener recommended
that theological students be encouraged to read *The German
Theology* and *The Imitation of Christ*.

In the seventeenth century numerous English devotional
writings were translated. Two works that went through many
printings were the Jesuit Robert Person's *Christian Directory*
(1582) and Anglican Bishop Joseph Hall's *Character of Virtues
and Vices* (1608), which were both translated into German and
then Swedish. Puritan works that were translated into

German and then into some of the Scandinavian languages included Lewis Bayly's *The Practice of Piety,* Richard Baxter's *The Saints' Everlasting Rest,* and, most perennially popular, John Bunyan's *The Pilgrim's Progress.*

6. *Devotional treatise.* Although definitions of devotional literature often limit it to popular works, there are also some writings that combine the formal, systematic character of a treatise intended for intellectuals with the direct, existential appeal to faith of a devotional work. Since much of the Lutheran tradition has placed a high value on theology and the intellectual life, it has produced some instances of the devotional treatise. A considerable number of such works were written by Søren Kierkegaard as *Edifying Discourses* published under his own name alongside his pseudonymous philosophical works. An example is *Purity of Heart is to Will One Thing* (1847). Another instance of this genre is Dietrich Bonhoeffer's *Nachfolge (The Cost of Discipleship)* (1937), which is drawn largely from his seminary lectures at Finkenwalde, and is both theologically demanding and existentially challenging.

Contemporary Practice

Lutheran devotional practice has traditionally been centred in the family. Luther expected the head of the family to lead in daily devotions, and this idea was followed in pious homes on the American frontier. The twentieth century brought widespread decline of this practice among European and North American Lutherans. In addition, those families that did have daily devotions came to rely increasingly on quarterly booklets whose daily readings are so brief as to provide little stimulation for meditation.

A related problem has been the heavy reliance of many first-world Lutherans on pre-written prayers and meditations, which may not foster genuine prayerful reflection. When Luther wrote out his explanations of the Ten Commandments, Apostles' Creed, and Lord's Prayer for Peter the barber, he warned him not merely to repeat Luther's words, but to let his mind and heart focus on the basic meanings. A great many first-world Lutherans have been schooled only to read written prayers and meditations without taking the time to ponder their deeper meaning. This generally is the practice at devotions for church gatherings such as meetings of women's circles and church boards. Many third-world Lutherans are not so restricted. For example, Tanzanian Lutherans pray more frequently and more spontaneously. When tea is served, the woman serving may offer a prayer and, when people are leaving on a journey, frequently someone prays.

The last several decades have seen a growing hunger among first-world Lutherans to learn how to pray and meditate. Interest in 'spirituality' has grown. Very often Lutherans with such a hunger have sought guidance at Roman Catholic, Anglican, or Orthodox retreat centres, and they have been reading books from various Christian and non-Christian sources. We have seen that in past generations Lutherans consulted devotional classics by non-Lutherans such as *The Imitation of Christ, The German Theology,* and *The Pilgrim's Progress* in addition to works by Lutherans. Such openness to the riches of other traditions is consistent with Lutheranism as an evangelical catholic tradition. At the Reformation, Lutherans did not carry on a wholesale rejection of the worship, devotional practice, and theology of the western Church and attempt a simple return to early Christianity. In addition to honouring the Bible, Lutherans respected the ancient teachings and practices that approached universal usage. The central criterion for the appropriation of all resources of belief and practice, of course, should be justification by grace through faith.

Largely unknown among contemporary Lutherans, though, are the many devotional writings from the Lutheran tradition. Of course, Arndt's *True Christianity* is challenging reading, but so are *The Imitation of Christ* and Teresa's *Interior Castle.* Some of the Lutheran classics deserve renewed attention.

In concluding this chapter, we may recall that we have reflected on Lutheran practices of attending to the Word in prayer and devotional literature. We turn next to attending to the Word in sacraments and physical symbols.

7. SACRAMENTS AND PHYSICAL SYMBOLS

In chapter one we observed that the ancient Latin phrase *lex orandi, lex credendi* may be interpreted in two ways. The more common interpretation is that the rule of prayer or worship is a norm for what is believed. This is the dominant way it has been understood in Roman Catholic theology. Yet grammatically the phrase can also be reversed, so that the rule of belief is a norm for Christian worship. This has been the predominant interpretation in Protestant theology, and we have seen this at work in the Lutheran tradition. We also noted that Geoffrey Wainwright argues that while these different orientations hold true in Catholicism and Protestantism, historically in both there also has been a mutual interaction between worship/prayer and doctrine. More broadly, I have argued that there is a mutual interaction between belief/doctrine and spiritual practice. Belief influences spiritual practice, and in turn persistent spiritual practice affects belief. In our contemporary cultural context of pick-and-choose spirituality, it is especially important to emphasize that spiritual practices do not exist like individual Lego bricks that can be combined with any number of other bricks to form any shape whatsoever. The meaning of any particular spiritual practice is closely associated with the context of beliefs and other practices in which it is embedded.

In this chapter we will focus on those rituals that Lutherans call sacraments, and we will see that Lutheran sacramental teaching and practice have important implications for the significance of other physical symbols in Lutheran spiritual practice. Sacraments are absolutely fundamental for

Lutheran spiritual practice, because it is through the sacraments and the Word of God in words that the Holy Spirit creates and strengthens faith. As *Augsburg Confession* Article 5 says, 'For through the Word and the sacraments as through instruments the Holy Spirit is given, who effects faith . . .' Lutherans strenuously rejected the idea that the Holy Spirit comes to human beings without external means.

Luther re-opened the related questions of the definition and number of sacraments, although the Lutheran Confessions give not altogether consistent answers to these questions. For more than the first thousand years of church history, there had been an indefinite number of things called sacraments. Much depended upon the definition, and Augustine was the first even to attempt definition. In the western Church the Council of Lyon (1274) recognized seven sacraments, and the Council of Florence (1439) affirmed seven, although it was not until the Council of Trent responded to the Protestant Reformation that the number was defined as no more and no less than seven.[1] In 1520 Luther raised again the question of definition and number. While medieval conceptions of a sacrament included being instituted by Christ, such institution could be explicit or implicit, that is, explicitly stated by Jesus as recorded in the Bible or implied by his teaching and action. Luther said a sacrament has an explicit divine Word of command and promise given in Scripture and an external sign. On this basis he recognized baptism and the Lord's Supper as sacraments, and for a while was uncertain about confession/absolution, because it lacked a distinctive external sign.

In the Lutheran Confessions baptism and the Lord's Supper are consistently affirmed as sacraments, while the practice of confession is strongly encouraged but usually not labelled a sacrament. The exception is in the *Apology of the Augsburg Confession,* article 13, where Melanchthon calls repentance/ absolution a sacrament and is also open to calling ordination with the laying on of hands a sacrament. Taking a similar view to Luther, Melanchthon defines a sacrament as a rite that has a divine command and promise, for as Word speaks to the ear, 'rite' speaks to the eye. So he praises Augustine for calling a sacrament a 'visible word'. Since confirmation, extreme unction, and marriage lack an explicit scriptural command and promise, they are not sacraments. Stretching his definition further, Melanchthon suggests prayer, alms, and afflictions might be called sacraments, since they all have God's command and promise. Yet, he says, agreement on the number of things called sacrament is not crucial, as long as those things which have God's command and promise are retained.

Since Lutherans consistently teach that the Holy Spirit gives and nurtures faith through both Word and sacrament, an integral dimension of Lutheran spiritual practice is attention to the sacraments. We shall now consider in turn baptism, the Lord's Supper, confession/absolution, and the broader implications of Lutheran sacramentality.

Baptism

Lutheran teaching and practice on baptism did not differ greatly from the tradition, but contrasted sharply with the view advanced by Anabaptists. Luther's discussion of baptism in two confessional writings, the *Small Catechism* and the *Large Catechism,* can be summed up in four points. First, in explanation of what baptism is and what its benefits are, Luther agrees with Augustine that it is not just plain water, but water connected with God's Word of command and promise. He cites Jesus' command to baptize disciples in Matthew 28:19 and the promise in Mark 16:16, 'The one who believes and is baptized will be saved'. On the basis of this promise, he teaches that baptism brings the benefit of salvation. Luther spells out the nature of salvation in various formulations in the *Large Catechism*, but his fullest statement of what baptism promises and brings is 'victory over death and the devil, forgiveness of sin, God's grace, the entire Christ, and the Holy Spirit with his gifts. In short, the blessings of baptism are so boundless that if our timid nature considers them, it may well doubt whether they could all be true.'[2] The Word of promise embodied in baptism is truly powerful, for in it God's own self is graciously present.

Second, in discussing the role of faith in baptism, Luther treads a path between an Anabaptist view and a mechanistic interpretation of the medieval affirmation that the sacraments work *ex opera operato*. Against the mechanistic understanding, he asserts that faith is necessary to receive the benefits of baptism. Against the view of Anabaptists and others he called 'enthusiasts', Luther insists that baptism is valid whether faith is present or not. Faith does not make or constitute baptism, but receives its benefits. What makes baptism is God's Word joined to water. So Luther claims the objective reality of God's grace in baptism, yet says faith is needed to receive that treasure. 'Without faith baptism is of no use, although in itself it is an infinite, divine treasure.'[3]

Luther also resists the Anabaptist and Spiritualist tendency to put all significance on the inner act of faith and to denigrate the importance of the external sign of water in baptism. For them baptism was generally considered an outward, public declaration of a previous inward act of faith, so they rejected infant baptism. Luther says the fact that God commands baptism means that it is not a matter to be taken lightly. Furthermore, the unsteady nature of faith means 'that faith must have something to believe – something to which it may cling and upon which it may stand.'[4] The external sign gives concreteness to God's Word. Because Luther recognizes that there is no direct biblical evidence for infant baptism, his defence of it includes appeal to the near universality of the practice for so many years. If God had not honoured the practice, there would be no Church today. Here he uses the rule of prayer to support the rule of belief.

Third, Luther stresses the lifelong significance of baptism. He rejects the idea that baptism is merely an event in the Christian's past. He blames St Jerome for the view that penance is the 'second plank' which Christians must use to help them swim ashore after they have lost through sin the safety of baptism. That long-prevalent view takes away the ongoing value of baptism. Instead in the *Small Catechism* Luther cites Paul's words in Romans 6:4, "'We were buried with Christ through baptism into death, so that, just as Christ was raised from the dead through the glory of the Father, we, too, are to walk in a new life.'" In both Catechisms he takes this to mean a daily turning from the old life of sin to new life in Christ. The ritual action of being dipped under the water and being drawn out again points to the ongoing power and effect of baptism – the slaying of the old Adam and the rising of the new person in Christ. 'Thus a Christian life is nothing else than a daily baptism, begun once and continuing ever after. For we must keep at it without ceasing, always purging whatever pertains to the old Adam, so that whatever belongs to the new creature may come forth.'[5] Luther is urging daily mindfulness of baptism in the sense of a daily spiritual movement of repentance, of turning from sin to Christ. 'Daily' does not mean literally once a day, but an ongoing, oft-repeated turning of the self from reliance upon human resources toward reliance upon God. He says that where faith is lacking, baptism is an unfruitful sign, but where faith grasps the inner meaning of this symbolic action, baptism is powerfully effective in human life.

Some people have understood this baptismal mindfulness only as confessing one's sin and receiving forgiveness each day, so the Christian life is viewed as running on the spot, as it were. But Luther says, 'This corruption must daily decrease so that the longer we live the more gentle, patient, and meek we become, and the more we break away from greed, hatred, envy, and pride.' He explains that where vices such as pride and greed are not resisted, they grow stronger day by day. 'On the other hand, when we become Christians, the old creature daily decreases until finally destroyed.' God's forgiving grace and transforming grace are both at work here, for wherever Christ and the Holy Spirit are present to faith, they effect both forgiveness and transformation.[6]

Overall, in respect to baptism Lutherans had very substantial agreement with Roman and Orthodox practice, but major differences with Anabaptist belief and practice.

Lord's Supper

The scope of differences between Lutheran practice and belief regarding the Lord's Supper and those of both Rome and some other reform movements was considerable, yet recent ecumenical discussions have revealed more agreement on several matters than was previously apparent.

Five points in Eucharistic belief and practice stand out. Several are addressed in Luther's concise answer in the *Small Catechism* to the question, 'What is the Lord's Supper?' Luther answers, 'It is the true body and blood of our Lord Jesus Christ under the bread and wine, instituted by Christ himself for us Christians to eat and to drink.'

1. The first point to note is that in Luther's view Christians are both to eat and drink. Already in 1520 he had attacked the Roman practice of giving the laity only the bread as being clearly contrary to the biblical words of Christ's institution. So Lutheran practice obviously differed from Roman usage in that laity were offered the cup. Other Protestant reform movements followed suit. This ceased to be an ecumenical issue when the Second Vatican Council liturgical reform permitted communion in both kinds.

2. The *Small Catechism* affirms a realistic understanding of Christ's presence, 'It is the true body and blood of our Lord Jesus Christ under the bread and wine.' the *Large Catechism* says 'in and under the bread and wine'. Common Lutheran usage has been to follow the *Formula of Concord* formulation 'in, with, and under'.[7] Not that Christ's presence is understood as locally enclosed in the bread and wine. The 'in, with, and under' of Lutheran doctrine points to the gracious mystery without trying to explain it. The Lutheran Confessions resist the Roman doctrine of transubstantiation as too much of a philosophical effort to explain the real presence.

Yet the Lutheran understanding is much closer to transubstantiation than to various 'sacramentarian' views. In an effort to ally the German and Swiss reform movements, Luther and Zwingli, along with others, met at the Marburg Colloquy in 1529 and agreed on fourteen articles of faith, but they could not agree on real presence. Over the centuries Lutherans, with few exceptions, have maintained a realistic view.[8] This despite the fact that the Zwinglian view of the Lord's Supper as a memorial that dramatically reminds believers of Christ's work on the cross generally seems more reasonable to the modern mind and is prevalent in most of Protestantism. Lutherans hold to their affirmation that 'it is the true body and blood of our Lord Jesus Christ under the bread and wine' chiefly because of two points of doctrine which would otherwise be at stake. One is the priority and objectivity of God's grace in the Lord's Supper. The common memorial view implies that Christ is present in the Lord's Supper only when and to the extent that the recipient is mindful of Christ. Christ's presence is subjective, in the human mind. Lutherans stress that Christ's presence in the Lord's Supper is objective. Christ is present to all recipients regardless of their faith or mental state, although only the believing obtain the benefits of Christ's gracious presence. The other thing at stake for Lutherans in asserting the real presence is the belief that people can be assured of God's gracious presence only where Jesus Christ is present, and that means the whole Jesus Christ, divine and human.

Practice as well as doctrine is an important testimony to Christ's real presence. In Wittenberg when Luther returned from hiding to restore order after Karlstadt's radical changes in worship, his retention of the presiding minister's act of elevating the consecrated elements was such a testimony. The elevation was eliminated there only in 1542, in order to bring Wittenberg practice in line with that of other Lutheran city and territorial churches in Germany. Another witness is the common but not universal Lutheran practice of kneeling to receive communion, an act that suggests special reverence.

Yet another is the practice of taking the consecrated elements out to those who are ill or shut in. However, Lutheran practice regarding proper use of consecrated bread and wine that are not consumed in communion has been uneven. Some have followed Melanchthon who apparently held that the sacramental union ended with the service or distribution of the sacrament to the ill, while others have followed Luther, who said whatever remains should be consumed and who chastised a pastor for mixing consecrated hosts with unconsecrated.[9]

Ecumenical discussions since the 1960s have come to acknowledge considerable convergence of Lutheran views with those of other major traditions, especially Roman Catholic, Anglican, and Reformed. For instance, the 1973 Lutheran–Reformed Leuenberg Concordat affirmed the objective presence of Christ in the Lord's Supper. Significant also is *Baptism, Eucharist and Ministry* (1982), a document of the Faith and Order Commission that included Roman Catholic representatives, which says, 'The Church confesses Christ's real, living and active presence in the eucharist.' The document acknowledges that differences remain on the relation between Christ's real presence and the sacramental elements.[10] The US Lutheran Catholic dialogue went further by affirming that Jesus Christ 'is present wholly and entirely, in his body and blood, under the signs of bread and wine', but says there is not yet full agreement on the prolongation of that presence and the language of transubstantiation.[11]

3. Another important element of Eucharistic belief and practice is expressed in Luther's *Small Catechism* statement that the Eucharist was instituted by Christ 'for us Christians to eat and drink'. This means it is a communal meal. Implicit here is rejection of two Roman practices – adoration of the elements and the private mass. Eucharistic adoration in several forms had become a very prominent part of medieval piety. By the thirteenth century, when people were receiving communion so seldom that the Fourth Lateran Council (1215) decreed the faithful must receive it at least once a year at Easter, adoration of consecrated elements at the elevation

along with ringing bells and genuflection had become the high point of the mass. Outside the mass, adoration of the reserved sacrament occurred mainly in four contexts: visiting the place in the church where the sacrament was retained; viewing the Blessed Sacrament in procession (especially on the Feast of Corpus Christi); gazing at the continuously exposed host in a monstrance; and being blessed in Solemn Benediction with the exposed host at the conclusion of a service.[12] So the Lutheran emphasis on Holy Communion as given for Christians to eat and drink, not to gaze upon, initiated a huge change in Eucharistic practice.

Luther's claim that the Lord's Supper is given for Christians to eat and drink also implicitly rejected the private mass. Joseph Jungmann says that the chief impetus for the private mass was people's desire for votive masses that dealt with their specific concerns (*vota*), especially for the dead. The private mass reached its most extreme form during the eighth and ninth centuries when masses were said by the priest alone, but then church legislation was introduced requiring at least one other person to be present, and in the thirteenth century it was stipulated this other person be a cleric.[13] In Lutheran practice the Lord's Supper is a communal action.

4. Lutheran rejection of the private mass has also been connected to a fourth issue: opposition to certain notions of the mass as a sacrifice. Luther vehemently attacked the belief that the mass is a sacrifice that frees from sin. In the *Smalcald Articles*, he calls it 'the greatest and most terrible abomination, as it directly and violently opposes justification by faith . . . For it is held that this sacrifice or work of the Mass . . . delivers people from sin . . .'[14] Fundamentally, what Luther is objecting to is the attitude of currying favour with God by offering the mass as a sacrifice. So in his Latin mass and German mass, Luther cut out language that spoke of the consecrated elements as a sacrifice. In Article 24 of the *Apology of the Augsburg Confession* Melanchthon distinguishes between two kinds of sacrifice – atoning sacrifice which frees from sin and Eucharistic sacrifice by which those

who are already reconciled to God give thanks and praise. While insisting that there has only been one true atoning sacrifice, that of Christ, he is willing to call the ceremony of the mass including the reception of the Lord's Supper a sacrifice of praise and thanks. Although most Lutheran churches have been very wary of using language of sacrifice or offering in connection with the consecrated elements, the Swedish Lutheran Church has been more open to it. Sixteenth-century Swedish reformer Laurentius Petri held that the mass is not only a sacrifice of thanks, but also may be called a sacrifice 'because it signifies or represents the sacrifice which Christ made upon the cross'.[15] This is close to what Roman Catholic theologians have said in recent dialogues with Lutherans: they understand the mass as a re-presenting of the one sacrifice of Christ, not an additional sacrifice. Nevertheless, this remains a difficult issue, for out of concern that the language can readily be misunderstood, Lutherans still are very cautious about speaking of sacrifice or offering in connection with the consecrated elements.

5. A final issue regarding belief and practice of the Lord's Supper is frequency of reception. As we noted, among the laity very infrequent reception had become common in the medieval period, although the mass occurred very often indeed. In Wittenberg Luther called for weekly Eucharist, and more often if people wished it. He also concludes his discussion of the Lord's Supper in the *Large Catechism* with an extended, heartfelt exhortation to receive communion frequently. He gives three main reasons. One is that Christ's words, 'Do this in remembrance of me', are a command and invitation that should not be ignored. Luther's remarks reveal part of his understanding of Christian freedom. People are now free from human commands in this matter such as the rule to receive at least once a year, but they are not free to despise Christ's command. In the background is an understanding of genuine freedom as wholeheartedly doing God's will. So disobedience to a divine command is a spurious freedom that fortifies bondage to sin. A second reason to receive

communion often is Christ's promise, ' "This is my body, given FOR YOU," "This is my blood, shed FOR YOU for the forgiveness of sins." These words . . . are not preached to wood or stone but to you and me . . . Ponder, then, and include yourself personally in the "You" so that he may not speak to you in vain.' The third reason for frequent communion is one's own need, and he offers several concrete suggestions for those who do not feel a need.[16]

Although Luther urged weekly celebration of the Lord's Supper and frequent reception, Lutheran practice on both counts has varied considerably. Lutheran territorial church orders generally followed Wittenberg in having a Sunday liturgy with communion. Detailed records for Leipzig reveal that communion was also offered once during the week at two different churches in the city.[17] During J.S. Bach's years there (1723–50) the yearly number of communicants at St Nicholas and St Thomas Churches averaged from 14,000 to 18,000 each. Later when rationalist clergy were installed, the number fell down to 3,000 by 1815. Frequency of the Eucharist also declined. In some churches, quarterly celebration – common in Reformed churches – was followed; in others monthly communion became standard. A reverse trend was promoted by leaders of the Neo-Lutheran movement in the nineteenth century and Lutherans in the Liturgical Movement of the twentieth century who stressed frequent communion as integral to evangelical catholic Lutheranism. In world Lutheranism there is still an ongoing movement toward weekly communion, so the importance of Holy Communion is being increasingly manifest not only in doctrine but also in practice.

Repentance and Absolution

The Lutheran tradition has generally followed Luther in not calling repentance and absolution a sacrament, yet Lutheran teaching and practice over the years have given mixed testimony to the importance of private confession. Luther and the

Lutheran Confessions affirm the great value of private confession. For instance, in his exhortation to confession in the *Large Catechism*, Luther recognized the practices of confessing to God alone and to one's neighbour alone (confessing to others that we have wronged them and asking their forgiveness) as well as private confession when a particular issue weighs on a person. Although part of evangelical liberty is freedom from church law requiring private confession, he says people's own need should impel them to seek it: 'Therefore, when I exhort you to go to confession, I am doing nothing but exhorting you to be a Christian.'[18]

Although Luther said private confession before communion should be encouraged but not required, in practice private confession and brief catechetical examination became standard preparation for receiving Holy Communion. In the *Formula Missae* (1523) Luther had stated that those wishing to receive communion should announce their desire to the pastor who then should examine them individually as to whether they knew the words of institution and could explain the benefits of the sacrament. This fits with Luther's stress upon Christ's words of promise as the chief part of the Eucharist. *Augsburg Confession* Article 25 points to this practice of examination and absolution before communion as a sign that confession has been retained. Such simple catechetical examination was not necessary each time a person came for communion, but was at the pastor's discretion. In Cologne confession occurred at a Saturday evening vespers confessional service. Frank Senn says this practice of the confessional service flourished for about two hundred years before fading.[19] In the nineteenth century some Lutherans made efforts to revive private confession, as have others more recently who stressed the evangelical catholic character of Lutheranism, but the practice has not become widespread.[20]

On the whole, Lutheran teaching and practice about confession and absolution have not been mutually consistent. Lutheran confessional teaching emphasizes the importance of confession and absolution. Indeed, the centrality of justification by faith means that confession of sin and absolution are core realities for Christians. For about two centuries Lutheran practice was somewhat in line with this teaching, with its inclusion of private confession before communion along with confession in public and to a neighbour. What has developed over time, though, is that private confession has become a practice of only a very few, and all that remains for most Lutherans is confession in public and to a neighbour. Luther said of private confession, 'This comes into play when some particular issue weighs on us or attacks us, eating away at us until we can have no peace nor find ourselves sufficiently strong in faith.'[21] While private confession, as Luther says, ought not be required, it should be readily available and encouraged. Here Lutheran practice should agree more fully with its doctrine.

Sacramentality

Richard McBrien, noted Roman Catholic theologian, says, 'A sacramental perspective is one that "sees" the divine in the human, the infinite in the finite, the spiritual in the material, the transcendent in the immanent, the eternal in the historical.' Over against this vision, he maintains, is the view, common in Protestantism, that God is 'wholly other'.[22] The Lutheran tradition has affirmed the sacramental perspective in many respects. One theological conflict related to the Eucharist centred around opposing beliefs by Reformed theologians, who held that the finite cannot contain the infinite, and by Lutherans, who affirmed that the infinite is in the finite. This sacramental perspective informs a Lutheran understanding of sacraments and Word.

Lutherans strongly opposed the belief of Zwingli, Anabaptists, and more radical segments of the Protestant Reformation that the sacraments are not objective means of grace, but simply rituals for remembrance or expression of a Christian's faith. The important thing in these so-called sacramentarian views was the inner experience of faith; the exterior rites are quite secondary. A key issue here is the mode of God's gracious dealings with humans. Lutherans have held that God's fundamental way of graciously approaching people is through outward means. In 1525 Luther expressed it this way:

> Now when God sends forth his holy gospel he deals with us in a twofold manner, first outwardly, then inwardly. Outwardly he deals with us through the oral word of the gospel and through material signs, that is, baptism and the sacrament of the altar. Inwardly he deals with us through the Holy Spirit, faith, and other gifts. But whatever their measure or order the outward factors should and must precede. The inward experience follows and is effected by the outward. God has determined to give the inward to no one except through the outward.[23]

Luther's central concern here is that placing the burden on people's remembrance and inner experience is to make a human action the key to the sacraments, whereas it is primarily God's action and gift. And God's gifts come to us through external means. The prime example of this is Jesus Christ, God present in a particular tangible human being. So in 1520 Luther spoke of Christ as the basic sacrament.[24] Although Lutheran Pietism put more stress on the subjective experience of faith, respect for the sacraments remained and has been strengthened through closer attention to Luther's writings and the confessional documents. So in dialogue with Catholics, Lutherans recognized a continued manifold presence of Christ in external things – in the Church as the body of Christ, the Word spoken in a human voice, and the visible word of sacraments.[25]

New currents of thought over the last century have prompted some fresh thinking by Lutherans about sacraments. The question of the number of sacraments, to which I alluded earlier in the chapter, is more open. Historical studies have shown that for over a millennium Christians had referred to a wide variety of things as sacraments. Augustine included not only baptism and eucharist, but such things as the sign of the cross, the salt used in baptism at that time, the baptismal font, the creed, and the Lord's Prayer. Furthermore, while Orthodox Churches have usually counted seven sacraments since the fifteenth century, there are Orthodox monks who still claim tonsure as a sacrament. 'Thus, the list of seven that generally prevails cannot be said to be as fixed in Orthodoxy as in Roman Catholicism. Orthodox theologians sometimes quip that the sacraments may be numbered variously as one, two, three, seven, nine – or 232.'[26] So in addition to baptism and the Lord's Supper, Lutheran Robert Jenson has spoken of penance, ordination, healing, and marriage as sacraments of return to baptism.[27]

Another current of thought has come from ecumenical scholarship. Roman Catholic theologians have spoken of sacramentality more broadly by noting the connections of the sacraments with the disclosure of God in and through various others things in nature and human life. While the sacraments are special occasions of personal encounter with God, they are not the exclusive means of divine personal presence. Lutheran practice is suggestive of belief in a broader notion of sacramentality. In church traditions there is a correlation between the importance of sacraments and the relative weight given other physical symbols. The prominence of icons, incense, candles, and other physical symbols in Orthodoxy is consistent with its emphasis on the seven sacraments. A similar correlation is evident in Catholicism. On the other hand, the fact that Quaker churches are extremely plain is linked to the fact that most of its communities do not have any sacraments. Similarly the lack of physical symbols in Evangelical-revivalist worship spaces is connected with these churches' teaching and practice on baptism and the Lord's Supper. In these traditions faith is nurtured overwhelmingly by words; physical symbols and the external signs of the sacraments are diminished. Lutheran practice regarding both sacraments and other physical symbols has been much closer to Orthodox and

Roman Catholic practice than to non-sacramental communities in Protestantism.

An appreciation of this broad meaning of sacramentality
has multiple ramifications for Lutheran spiritual practice and
teaching. One is recognition that physical symbols other than
the sacramental signs often play a significant role in people's
spiritual practice. A case in point is the powerful influence
that images of Jesus often have in people's lives. Based upon
his study of reactions of people, including many Lutherans, to
Warner Sallman's *Head of Jesus* David Morgan says, 'Many
have asserted that Sallman's image proactively shapes one's
inner life into the likeness of Christ. More than merely curb-
ing certain behaviors . . . the *Head of Christ* has been credited
with the power to inspire the imitation of its subject.'[28] Many
Lutherans could testify also to the influence of an altar paint-
ing or a stained glass window in a church or to a cross on their
desk. Such physical symbols often play a significant role in the
devotional life of an individual, family, or community. To be
sure, these symbols do not come with God's command and
promise, as do the sacraments, and they are subject to misuse.
Artist Theodore Prescott points out that for the last hundred
years popular pictures of Jesus have not been solidly rooted in
the Church's traditions about him, but have been created and
marketed more to suit the preference of individuals.[29]
However, the fact that such physical symbols can be manipu-
lated and misused does not mean they all should be abolished.
Rather, critique and fresh inspiration from the Word is in
order.

Another dimension of broad sacramentality is Christian
faith embodied in daily life. Christian faith is incarnational.
Just as this faith is nurtured through the external means of
audible word and tangible sacrament, so faith is expressed
and shaped by concrete patterns of action in everyday life. In
a culture that relegates religion to the private sphere, David
Yeago has adopted the usage of Neo-Lutheran Wilhelm Loehe
in speaking of 'sacramental Lutheranism' as a corporate practice that is rooted in Eucharistic worship and reaches out to

sanctify the material world by taking all things into God's service. 'This is the priestly vocation of God's people, in contemporary terms its "mission": not simply to "save souls" but to redeem creation by fashioning on the earth a new kind of embodied life together, centered in worship.'[30] So after examining Lutheran belief and practice on baptism, Eucharist, confession/absolution, and some other aspects of a broader sacramentality, we will turn our attention in the next chapter to an incarnational understanding of faith in daily life.

8. FAITH IN DAILY LIFE

We have understood spirituality as a faith expressed in and nurtured by certain practices. We began by focusing on major elements in Lutheran faith – its understanding of the human predicament, justification by grace through faith, and authoritative sources of wisdom. Then we considered the core practices concerned with the Word of God, prayer, and sacraments, all of which are clearly religious practices. Now we will look at practices that are not so obviously religious, but may also express and nurture Christian faith – social ethical activity. We begin with the predominant faith perspective within which these practical matters have been understood in the Lutheran tradition – the so-called two kingdoms doctrine.

Two Kingdoms

Luther does not articulate a tightly knit doctrine of two kingdoms, but responds to a variety of situations and issues by distinguishing between dual realities with a fairly coherent set of ideas. The cluster of ideas associated with the two kingdoms in Luther's thought has precursors in the biblical distinction between the children of light and the children of darkness as well as in Augustine's conception of two cities.

On the one hand, there is the kingdom of the world or temporal sphere in which God as Creator and Preserver works to sustain order and some degree of justice in the world. God does this through two orders of creation: government and family. Here God governs by requirements, custom, and law – formal and informal, legal and moral. In some contexts Luther speaks of this activity purely in negative terms, as restraining evil. In such contexts civil law and authorities are described as chains binding a wild beast that otherwise would break out and destroy human society. Yet Luther also affirms a positive role for the orders of creation, for parents and all authorities in society are to use their position for the benefit of others and thereby share in God's work of sustaining human life.

On the other hand, there is the spiritual kingdom wherein God rules by the gospel and faith. The institution through which the gospel is mediated is the Church. Here through the external means of grace God rules in the human heart by faith in Christ and love for other people. Insofar as believers live in Christ, they need no constraint by law and external compulsion, because they willingly and gladly do more than the law and police require.[1]

The main function of the two kingdoms 'doctrine' is to distinguish between two different yet related realities. One distinction Luther makes is between two modes of divine activity – creation and redemption, law and gospel. Here Luther tends to speak of *two governments*. God governs through both law and gospel, but it is vital to observe the distinction between these two modes of divine activity. Divine governance through law works by requirement and compulsion. So the civil use of law and police exerts pressure on people to do good. In the family parents set rules for children, and may penalize a child for misbehaving. In the workplace being a truck driver or sales person entails certain requirements in performance, and failure to meet them brings a cost. So in a variety of ways limits to behaviour in society are set by laws and punishments. God rules here through law, in order to sustain human life. Divine governance through the gospel works by redirecting the human heart to faith in God and love toward others. God governs in both ways, but it's crucial to observe the difference.

A second distinction of the two kingdoms idea is between social institutions which should not be confused. In this context Luther tends to speak of *two kingdoms*. By the early sixteenth century there had been a long history of the institutions of

Church and State becoming mixed. Pope and bishops were secular rulers over considerable territories, and secular rulers, including the Holy Roman Emperor, often claimed authority in religious matters. In addition, in the sixteenth century some radical reformers, whom Luther called 'enthusiasts', sought to make civil society conform to Christian faith and the gospel. Other radicals taught that Christians should withdraw from actively supporting civil government; they should not serve as judges or police officers and should not ever engage in war. Over against these various ways of relating Church and civil society, Luther's two kingdoms doctrine called for distinction between civil society and church while maintaining that Christians should not separate from responsibilities in civil government. This distinction is also articulated in Articles 16 and 28 of the *Augsburg Confession*.

Third, the two kingdoms teaching sometimes distinguishes between two spheres of moral behaviour by Christians. In the realm of interpersonal relations, Christians are to follow Christ's teaching of not resisting evil. If someone strikes them or takes some of their possessions, Christians are not to strike back or use force to regain their possessions (Matt. 5:38-41). Here Christians are to manifest love of neighbour in the most radical sense. However, in more public situations, they should manifest their love for others whose life and property is threatened by using force to defend the life and property of those people. Luther said that out of concern for others, a Christian could be a judge and, if needed, even serve as a hangman. The Christian could also participate in a just war.[2]

This conception of two kingdoms has been the framework for most Lutheran thinking about social ethics, both in the social roles of everyday life as one's vocation and in wider social ethical activity. We begin with Luther's idea of vocation.

Vocation

Vocation or calling is a major biblical concept. Most often in the Greek Old Testament (Septuagint) and New Testament, 'calling' (*kaleo, klesis,* and related terms) refers to God's call to faith. In his lecture on Genesis 17:9 Luther designates this as the universal or general call. But in 1 Corinthians 7:20 Paul says, 'Let each of you remain in the *klesis* in which you were called', and he goes on to advise slaves to remain slaves and the unmarried to remain unmarried. Some contemporary scholars translate *klesis* here as 'condition'; others along with Luther take it to mean a station or place in society. Thus, according to Luther, in addition to the general call to faith, for each person there is a divine call to serve other people in and through a particular social station and its duties.

The distinction between the temporal kingdom and spiritual kingdom is part of the framework for Luther's thinking about vocation. As Creator and Sustainer God works through three orders or estates in society – the church (pastors, sextons, and the like), the family or household (husbands, wives, parents, children, single people, servants), and civil government (princes, judges, police, and subjects). It's not clear how economic activity fits into this scheme, but given the family-owned nature of such enterprises at that time, farms and businesses are likely included within the household.[3] Everyone has a station, for everyone has a position in a family/household and civil society. Indeed, many have multiple stations, for a person might have a social role in family, civil society, and church. Anyone who carries out their constructive roles competently and conscientiously thereby helps others. God does not directly feed a baby, build a house, or defend the helpless against robbers, but God effects such things indirectly through parents, carpenters, and police. These, Luther calls, the 'masks' of God. In one way or another, everyone participates in God's temporal kingdom.[4]

It's a different matter, says Luther, with God's spiritual kingdom and government:

> in which God Himself dwells, reigns, and works through
> His Word and Spirit toward a spiritual, eternal life. For
> this is God's own realm: to baptize, to preach the Gospel,

to administer the Sacrament, to console and strengthen timid and grieving consciences, to terrify and punish the wicked with excommunication, to perform works of love and mercy, and to endure the cross.[5]

Participation in the spiritual kingdom includes carrying out the responsibilities of one's station with faith active in love and so recognizing oneself as a mask of God. Vocation is for service. The purpose of one's calling to a particular social station is to serve others. God calls husbands and wives to help their spouse, princes to care for their subjects, and manual labourers to use their tools to aid their neighbours. It's not enough, though, simply to be good-hearted. Competence is also important. Parents should know how to change a nappy, princes should be able to make sound judgements, and carpenters should be skilled at their craft. Natural ability, hard work, and good thinking are valuable instruments for faith. So equipped, faith that intimately connects one to Christ is the heartbeat of vocation.

Luther's thinking about vocation was both innovative and conservative. His innovation in respect to vocation was to teach that all constructive social roles are equally good in God's eyes. This contrasted with the accepted medieval notion that life as a monk, nun, or priest under the evangelical counsels of celibacy, poverty, and obedience is a holier vocation than life in the secular realm. Whereas the medieval idea was that the calling to monastic life was holier than a calling to some secular station, Luther said all constructive callings are equal in God's eyes. In fact, he discouraged people of his time from taking monastic vows, because the vows were usually overlaid with spiritually dangerous ideas about winning God's favour through a supposedly higher life. Mindful of this warning, though, today there exist a few Lutheran monastic communities such as the Augustinian Sisters of the Casteller Ring in Erfurt, Germany and Saint Augustine's House in Oxford, Michigan, USA. In any case, Luther initiated a profound and far-reaching shift in focus of spiritual life and practice – from concentration on a reputedly higher pattern under the evangelical counsels to Christ-centred existence in ordinary daily life. This change has the potential to invest ordinary life with profound meaning.

While Luther's thinking about vocation was in some respects innovative, in other ways it was conservative. Luther had a hierarchical understanding of social institutions. Husbands are in charge of the family, masters are over their servants, and princes govern subjects. He also thought of these institutions as static. He admonished people to remain in their station, not to seek another or better one. More recent Lutheran interpreters have abandoned such hierarchical and static thinking, while upholding the essentials of Luther's idea of vocation.

In a Lutheran understanding, Christian spirituality includes the daily performance of one's vocation(s) as a spiritual practice. Christian faith is not only manifest in religious practices such as corporate worship, meditation, and retreat, but is also *expressed* in the faithful performance of one's duties day to day. This has been a persistent theme in the Lutheran tradition. However, another aspect of vocation in spirituality has not been commonly recognized, namely, that faithful performance of one's vocation also tends to *shape and nurture* one's faith and moral character. The apostle Paul found this to be true. He says,

> I have learned to be content with whatever I have. I know what it is to have little, and I know what it is to have plenty. In any and all circumstances I have learned the secret of being well-fed and of going hungry, of having plenty and of being in need. I can do all things through him who strengthens me. (Phil. 4:11b-13)

Here Paul speaks of what he has learned through long experience in his calling as an apostle. He has learned to be content with whatever he has, and he has learned the secret of being well-fed and of going hungry. His vocation as apostle and missionary for Christ has shaped him.

It's likely that anyone who follows a vocation for an extended time will find something similar. For example, my role as husband to Marion for over forty years has helped me become more understanding and appreciative of another person different from me and increasingly grateful for the gift of her love. My role as father to three children has fostered, among other qualities, thankfulness, patience, readiness to praise, and slowness to criticize. My work as a college professor for thirty-two years tended to make me a better listener, more understanding of student needs and difficulties, and – most slowly of all – more accepting of colleagues with whom I had major differences. In other words, God not only nurtures faith through the 'means of grace' – Word and sacrament – but God may also shape and nurture faith in and through a person's everyday callings.

Wider Social Ethics

Lutheran thinking about wider social ethics has been going through considerable ferment ever since the Second World War. Widespread support of German Lutherans for Hitler and the passivity of most of them toward his Jewish policies and domination of the Church triggered re-examination of Lutheran social ethical thought and especially the two kingdoms 'doctrine'. The stance of most German Lutherans toward Hitler during his reign was the outcome of a long historical development.

Luther's own response to a range of social issues with his two kingdoms dialectic varied considerably. Franklin Sherman identifies three functions of the two kingdoms framework in Luther's thought. The first function is to *distinguish* – between two modes of God's activity, between the institutions of Church and State, and between two spheres of human activity (the interpersonal and public). We discussed these aspects of the distinguishing function above. A second function is to *limit*. In his 1523 treatise *On Temporal Authority: To What Extent It Should Be Obeyed*, Luther advises people not to obey an order by some civil authorities to hand over Luther's books. He uses the two kingdoms idea to assert that civil rulers have no authority over spiritual matters. The limiting function also cuts the other way, for the Church should not try to dictate answers to temporal problems. For example, the Church should not try to impose a Christian morality of love on everyone. Rather, Christians should contribute to a common, rational quest for justice. This points to a third function of the two kingdoms idea, the *prophetic*. The Church and its preachers have a responsibility to speak out for justice in society. Luther did this on numerous occasions, for he often publicly criticized the actions of civil rulers. He also tried to deal constructively with the vast social changes occurring from the collapse of monasteries by advancing a proposal that a community assist the poor through a common chest and by urging city authorities to replace monastic schools with schools for both boys and girls. Philip Melanchthon even proposed an entire system of education.[6]

Luther's record, though, includes two stances for which he has rightly been criticized and which laid some groundwork for what happened under Hitler. One was his stance on forceful resistance to civil authority. In 1525 when peasants sought better conditions, Luther expressed sympathy with their complaints. But when they took up arms, he called on the rulers in severe terms to put down the rebellion. Later when the Lutheran princes were threatened with war by the emperor, Luther supported their right to fight on the grounds that princes could resist their overlord. But he saw no place for ordinary subjects to rebel against legitimate civil authority. To be sure, interpreters of the Word should speak out against injustice, but he drew the line at verbal opposition. In addition to this rejection of forceful resistance to political authority Luther started a tradition of rulers dominating the Lutheran Church in their territory. In 1521 when the pope and most bishops were opposing reform of the Church, Luther urged the princes to lead such reform. Rulers became, as it were, emergency bishops. By the end of the sixteenth century the organization of the Lutheran churches was solidly under the control of their prince. So, through both design and historical circumstance, Luther fostered a conservative stance toward political authority.

The second issue for which Luther has received severe criticism is his recommendations regarding Jews. Although in a 1523 treatise Luther opposed mistreatment of Jews in hope that good treatment would encourage them to become Christians, in several writings from the last decade of his life Luther became increasingly harsh toward them. In 1543 he recommended that Jews be excluded from the community, their holy books seized, and their synagogues burned. Like Ezra and Nehemiah who wanted to expel foreign women from the post-exilic Jewish community, Luther thought Jews did not belong among Christians. Scholars point to factors that very likely influenced this change of attitude in Luther: decline in health after late 1536 which made him much more irascible, his belief in Christ's imminent return, and the credence he gave to reports that Jews were proselytizing. Nevertheless, for many people Luther has become a symbol of anti-Semitism.[7]

The long-term impact of Luther's varied responses to diverse social issues was to approve a conservative stance toward political authority. Even though Luther was a rebel against church authorities and often spoke out on public issues in opposition to civil authorities, the outcome was that Lutheran churches were dominated by temporal rulers.

This arrangement was not seriously challenged by Lutheran Orthodox theologians, who followed Luther in speaking of three estates – Church, State, and family. As in Luther's two kingdoms perspective God rules through the gospel in the Church, on the one hand, and through law in State and family, on the other hand. Although Orthodox theologians said civil authorities should protect the Church and not interfere in its internal doctrinal or disciplinary affairs, the reality in many cases was just the opposite.[8] Franklin Sherman points out two shifts from Luther in the social ethics of Orthodoxy, 'The note of joy in the goodness of the created order recedes . . . behind the heavy emphasis on the ordering or restrictive functions.

And the division of labor between the three estates is so inter-preted as to undercut the prophetic function of the church.[9]

Although Lutheran Pietists were very active in charitable works and in creating their own institutions for education, mental retardation, and refugee work, Sherman says that in effect they had a one kingdom doctrine. They focused wholly on God working through believers who then have an impact on society. Luther's belief that God also works through secular structures was given little attention.[10] This approach was followed in large measure also by the Inner Mission under the leadership of the German Lutheran pastor J.H. Wichern (1808–81). This movement, which spread to other Lutheran countries, combined social and evangelistic work in an effort to help those dislocated by industrialization and alienated from the Church. Leaders of the Neo-Lutheran theological move-ment such as Wilhelm Loehe also interpreted the two kingdoms idea in a way that stressed the Church's indirect influence on the political order through shaping the faith of Christians. More direct challenge to political authorities by church leaders was thought inappropriate.[11] This approach fit comfortably with the Enlightenment way of seeing religious faith as a private matter, and it prepared the way in Germany for widespread non-resistance to Hitler.

Since the Second World War Lutherans have looked afresh at social ethics, and have sought to make connections between Christian faith and social questions both in public life and theology. In public life German Lutheran churches have estab-lished a number of Evangelical Academies like the one at Loccum near Hannover. On these monastery grounds, leaders in medicine, law, government, management, labour, and other fields meet with church leaders to discuss critical questions in both formal and informal settings. The Academy also produces publications on a variety of ethical issues.

In theology while some Lutherans drawn to liberation theol-ogy have favoured the abandonment of a two kingdoms view, most have called for a re-interpretation that does not separate God's two ways of governing. The heart of a sound two kingdoms perspective, they say, is the conviction that God acts in the world in two distinct yet dynamically related ways identified as creation and redemption or law and gospel. These two forms of divine activity will become united in the ultimate future, but until then are distinguishable.

An example of a revised two kingdoms approach is offered by American ethicist Robert Benne. Using H. Richard Niebuhr's classic characterization of Luther's social ethics as Christ and culture in paradox, Benne calls it the 'paradoxical vision'. Benne rejects a dualistic understanding as 'a Lutheran heresy' which separated the two dimensions of God's rule. He understands a paradox as two statements that appear to be contradictory, but are ultimately both true. So the two aspects of God's ruling activity are to be held in tension until God unites them at the fulfilment of human history.

This stress on persistent tension between Christ and culture differentiates the Lutheran stance from the other stances delineated by H. Richard Niebuhr. The Christ *against* culture posture of the Amish, for example, sees the two realities as not only separate, but largely alien to one another. The Christ *of* culture outlook, such as that of nineteenth-century liberal Protestants, tends to merge Christian faith with culture. The characteristic Roman Catholic stance has been Christ and culture *in synthesis*, that is, to see how the elements of goodness and grace in a culture may find fulfilment in the grace of Christ. In the Reformed attitude of Christ *transforming* culture, the aim is to renew society in a way analogous to sanctification of the individual. While all of these views distinguish two aspects of God's activity, they differ in the degree to which they think those two aspects can become unified within history. The Roman Catholic and Reformed have a relatively positive opinion on this question, although not as optimistic as the Christ of culture stance.

In effect, what had happened to Lutherans for much of modern history was to regard Christ and the social ethical dimensions of culture as separate, although not necessarily opposed or alien to each other. What most Lutherans like

Robert Benne have tried to do since the Second World War is place Christian faith and social ethical issues in conversation with each other. Benne says the paradoxical vision recognizes, on the one hand, God's active rule through law in its many forms. Although most earlier Lutheran interpretations had emphasized the negative power of law and social institutions as dikes against the expression of sin, Benne follows certain nineteenth- and twentieth-century Scandinavian theologians such as Gruntvig, Wingren, and Aulen in stressing the positive, constructive role of law and social institutions in advancing justice in human life. Benne says,

> God, through many agencies, cajoles the world toward more expansive and fulfilling relations among beings. Love is developed, justice is extended and refined, and the world is made a better place to live. God operates through "masks" to get this work done. Many of these masks are not recognizably Christian or even religious.[12]

On the other hand, Benne says the Church must stay true to its unique mission of proclaiming and being faithful to its core vision. This vision centres in the gospel of God's grace in Jesus Christ, and includes also key teachings summarized in the classic creeds and fundamental moral teachings. When it comes to applying this core vision to specific social issues, though, there is ample room for disagreement among Christians. As examples of this approach, Benne cites some statements on ethical issues coming from the Evangelical Lutheran Church in America and its predecessor bodies. These social statements have had three purposes: to instruct individuals on the issues under consideration without binding them to a certain stance, to commit the institution of the ELCA in certain ways, and to make a public witness to the society.

Benne sees the clear distinction between the Church's core gospel message and particular social programmes as a safeguard against identifying God's will too closely with a particular social ideology and movement, whether it be Marxism, democracy, feminism, or whatever. He regards this tendency to identify a particular social movement too closely with God's will as a danger with the Reformed transformation-ist approach to social ethics, which has been dominant in United States history.

Those Lutherans drawn to liberation theology place less emphasis on tension between the two kingdoms and more emphasis on seeing how the kingdom of God can inform life in the temporal realm. This perspective has been especially influential among Lutherans in developing countries, and is succinctly expressed in this quote from Rudelar Bueno de Faria from El Salvador on the Department for World Service web-page, 'Hope continues within those who visualize a different world. As the Department for World Service, we cannot but strengthen all efforts that seek to plant signs of the kingdom of God on earth.' Liberation theology has also been attractive to many Lutherans from wealthy nations who have been closely involved in work with disadvantaged people at home or abroad. American ethicist Larry Rasmussen also finds support for such a stance in Dietrich Bonhoeffer. In any case, discussion about social ethics and the two kingdoms 'doctrine' is ongoing among Lutherans.

Just as vocation is a means both to express and nurture Christian faith, so also with wider social ethical activity. The Lutheran World Federation, a communion of most Lutheran churches, has a Department for World Service with a record of work with refugees, victims of natural disasters, and the poor that began after the Second World War and now co-operates with other agencies in relief work and sustainable develop-ment in many countries around the world. Such work *expresses* the faith of those who participate. The Department for World Service webpage quote from the representative from El Salvador continues, 'We are justified by grace and faith and this means: service to others.' In addition, such work also tends to *nurture and shape* the faith of those directly involved. For instance, privileged Lutherans from prosperous nations who work with the poor in developing nations frequently find that their own faith has been deepened and broadened in unexpected ways.

We began the discussion in this chapter by recalling our basic conception of 'spirituality'. Frequently spirituality is taken as referring to religious practices, for some people even private religious practices. We have understood spirituality more broadly as a faith that is expressed and nurtured by certain practices. While religious practices certainly play an essential role in Lutheran spirituality, moral action also has an indispensable part. Indeed, in this realm there is a comparable relation between faith and practice. Here there is debate among Lutherans of how Christian faith should frame moral action. The predominant ethical framework has been the two kingdoms 'doctrine', but a contemporary minority wants to revise that in the more prophetic direction of liberation theology. Lutherans agree on the notion of vocation as God's call to serve others in and through one's social roles in family and work, and they agree broadly that Christian persons and communities have responsibilities in larger social circles of local community, nation, and world. Christian faith will find expression in public life, and in turn that ethical activity over time nurtures and shapes Christian faith.

EPILOGUE

Lutheran spirituality is a particular way of being spiritual, of actualizing that God-given human potential to affirm meaning in life, and it is a particular way of being religious and Christian. Lutheran spirituality shares a great deal with historic Christianity going back to Scripture and the traditions of the ancient Church. It is a catholic spirituality that espouses beliefs and practices that are universal in the sense that they are supported both by Scripture and long-term, widespread usage in the Church. Thus, Lutheran spirituality has much in common with the Roman Catholic, Orthodox, and Anglican traditions, and with these traditions is strongly sacramental.

Lutheran spirituality also has much in common with many other Protestant traditions, such as insistence on the authority of Scripture above that of tradition and recognition of two rituals as sacraments. Lutheran spirituality is evangelical, for the key criterion for its theology and practice is the gospel, the centre of which is articulated in doctrinal terms as justification by grace alone through faith alone. What the doctrinal language of justification refers to is the faith relationship with Christ. In this relationship, as Luther says, faith trusts God's promises, honours and obeys God, and unites the believer with Christ.

This faith relationship with Christ brings a spiritual freedom over sin, death, and the devil, for even though the believer is assailed by these evil powers, Luther says, 'There is nothing so good and nothing so evil but that it shall work together for good to me, if only I believe.'[1] In this faith relationship there is both freedom from the guilt of sin through God's forgiveness and freedom from the domination of sin through God's transforming grace that resists sin. The power does not lie in a subjective act of believing, but in Christ present in and with the believer. This Christ-centred faith relationship is the heart of Lutheran spirituality. Such faith is expressed and nurtured by Word and sacrament, for the Lutheran Confessions have the sacramental conviction that God's redemptive grace is communicated through the outward means of Word and sacrament. The core spiritual practices are ways of attending to Word and sacrament and living out the faith in daily life.

While the faith and practice of Lutherans has a great deal that is widely shared among Christian traditions, Lutheran spirituality was born amidst controversy on several fronts over certain points in theology and spiritual practice. As we have seen, Lutherans rejected a number of spiritual practices that had become common in western Christianity on the grounds that they lacked scriptural support or conflicted with justification by grace through faith. The principal way Lutherans interpreted *lex orandi, lex credendi* was that the rule of faith is a norm for prayer. In many of these controversies a major Lutheran concern was that people's spiritual freedom was being compromised by confusing regulations made by ecclesiastical leaders with God's law.

There has never been uniformity in Christian spirituality. Already in the New Testament writings diversity is evident within unity of confession of faith in Jesus the Messiah. Differences in time, place, and circumstances often call forth somewhat different responses. This has been true also within the Lutheran community. We have seen how the faith and practice of the early Lutheran reformers was received and adapted by Lutheran Orthodoxy, Pietism, and later movements such as Neo-Lutheranism. The chief unifying factors within the Lutheran tradition of spirituality have been the Lutheran Confessions and the writings of Martin Luther. In addition to feeding regularly on Scripture like other Christians, Lutherans have leaders who repeatedly return to the Lutherans Confessions and Martin Luther for guidance.

The dialogue between the Lutheran confessional tradition and contemporary culture has already entered a new phase. European and North American forms of Lutheran spirituality will increasingly be supplemented and transformed by African, Latin, and Asian forms. While Lutheran spiritual practice will continue to stress attention to Word and sacrament and living out faith in daily life, the concrete forms of doing so will likely change.

Participation in ecumenical conversations over the last century has fostered among most Lutherans both a clearer understanding of their own strengths and greater appreciation for the gifts of other traditions. On the one hand, the Lutheran emphasis on justification by grace through faith is an extremely valuable contribution to all of Christianity, for it encourages deeper reflection by all on the Christian message of salvation. On the other hand, moving beyond denominational isolation has helped reawaken Lutherans to the riches of faith and spiritual practice in other Christian traditions. For the foreseeable future, the catholic evangelical voice of Lutherans will continue to be an important part of the whole Christian choir.

NOTES

1. Faith, Practice and History

1. Geoffrey Wainwright, *Doxology: The Praise of God in Worship, Doctrine, and Life* (New York: Oxford University Press, 1980), 218-50.
2. *ibid.*, 251-71.
3. Cited in Martin Brecht, *Martin Luther*, vol. 1, *His Road to Reformation 1483-15*, tr. James L. Schaaf (Philadelphia: Fortress, 1985), 453. My account of Luther at the Diet of Worms is based upon Brecht.
4. *ibid.*, 460.
5. *ibid.*, 474.
6. *ibid.*, 125-8.
7. *ibid.*, 156.
8. *ibid.*, 176-83, 190-2.
9. *ibid.*, 221-37. See Luther's 1545 Preface to his Latin Writings, LW, 34: 336-7.
10. Martin Brecht maintains the theological shift occurred somewhere between spring and autumn 1518: *ibid.*, 229-31. James M. Kittelson argues that Luther's new understanding of justification came in late 1518 or early 1519, yet earlier developments already undercut medieval piety: *Luther the Reformer: The Story of the Man and His Career* (Minneapolis: Augsburg, 1986), 94-100, 134-5.
11. Kittelson, *Luther the Reformer*, 182-3. Martin Brecht, *Martin Luther*, vol. 2, *Shaping and Defining the Reformation 1521-1532*, tr. James L. Schaaf (Minneapolis: Fortress, 1990), 59-61.
12. *BC*, 5.
13. The distinction among Anabaptists, Spiritualists, and Evangelical Rationalists within the Radical Reformation is the widely accepted contribution of George Huntston Williams, *The Radical Reformation*, 3rd edn (Kirksville: Sixteenth Century Journal Publishers, 1992), 14-17.
14. Frank C. Senn, *Christian Liturgy: Catholic and Evangelical* (Minneapolis: Fortress, 1997), 517-29.
15. Short selections from these three works appear in Eric Lund (ed.),

Documents from the History of Lutheranism 1517-1750 (Minneapolis: Fortress, 2002), 258-71.

16. Philip Jacob Spener, *Pia Desideria*, tr. and ed. Theodore Tappert (Philadelphia: Fortress, 1964), 87-117.

17. Senn, *Christian Liturgy: Catholic and Evangelical*, 499.

18. Eric W. Gritsch, *Fortress Introduction to Lutheranism* (Minneapolis: Fortress, 1994), 69-78.

2.   Sin and God's Prior Initiative

1. *BC*, 6.

2. H. George Anderson, T. Austin Murphy, and Joseph A. Burgess (eds.), *Justification by Faith: Lutherans and Catholics in Dialogue VII* (Minneapolis: Augsburg, 1985), 19-20.

3. Richard Kieckhefer, 'Major Currents in Late Medieval Devotion', in *Christian Spirituality: High Middle Ages and Reformation*, ed. Jill Raitt (New York: Crossroad, 1987), 75-108.

4. *Joint Declaration on the Doctrine of Justification* (Grand Rapids: Eerdmans, 2000), 17.

5. Paul R. Sponheim, 'Sin and Evil', in *Christian Dogmatics*, ed. Carl E. Braaten and Robert W. Jenson, vol. 1 (Philadelphia: Fortress, 1984), 410-22.

6. *BC*, SD, article 1, 11.

7. Johann Arndt, *True Christianity*, tr. Peter Erb (New York: Paulist, 1979), Bk I, Chap. 2, p. 33.

8. Robin Maas and Gabriel O'Donnell, *Spiritual Traditions for the Contemporary Church* (Nashville: Abingdon, 1990), 15.

9. Anthony de Mello, *Sadhana: A Way to God* (St Louis: Institute of Jesuit Sources, 1978), 10.

10. Philip Sheldrake, *Befriending Our Desires* (Notre Dame: Ave Maria Press, 1994), 25-6.

11. Augustine, *Confessions*, in *Basic Writings of Saint Augustine*, ed. W.J. Oates, vol. 1 (New York: Random House, 1948), 3.

12. Sheldrake says, 'At the level of deep desires, any distinction between what we desire and the desires with which God gifts us actually begins to blur' (*Befriending Our Desires*, 22-3). However, this seems to be the gifts bestowed in our creation as image of God, whereas Lutherans would see such positive desires as fruits of redemption.

3.   Justification by Grace through Faith

1. H. George Anderson, T. Austin Murphy, Joseph A. Burgess (eds.), *Justification by Faith: Lutherans and Catholics in Dialogue VII* (Minneapolis: Augsburg, 1985), 19.

2. *ibid.*, 35.

3. Johann Arndt, *True Christianity*, tr. Peter Erb (New York: Paulist, 1979), Foreword, 21.

4. *ibid.*, 24.

5. F. Ernest Stoeffler, *German Pietism During the Eighteenth Century* (Leiden: Brill, 1973), 8-9.

6. Dietrich Bonhoeffer, *The Cost of Discipleship*, rev. edn (New York: Collier, 1963), 45-8.

7. *Joint Declaration on the Doctrine of Justification* (Grand Rapids: Eerdmans, 2000), 15.

8. *ibid.*, 18.

9. *ibid.*, 19.

10. Tuoma Mannermaa, 'Theosis as a Subject of Finnish Luther Research', *Pro Ecclesia*, 4, no. 1:37-48.

11. Eric W. Gritsch, 'Did Luther Teach "Theosis"? Issues and Answers from Finnish Luther Research and Pauline Studies', unpublished paper given at the Lutheran Theological Society of North America, 24 Nov. 1991, 11.

12. James M. Kittelson, 'Contemporary Spirituality's Challenge to *Sola Gratia*', *Lutheran Forum*, 19 (Winter 1995), 373-6; 382-4.

13. *LW*, 31:349-52; Lull, 601-4.

14. Scott Hendrix, 'Martin Luther's Reformation of Spirituality', *Lutheran Quarterly*, 13:1, 255.

15. Johann Gerhard, *Sacred Meditations*, tr. C.W. Heisler (Philadelphia: Lutheran Publication Society, 1896), 65.

16. Heinrich Schmid, *The Doctrinal Theology of the Evangelical Lutheran Church*, tr. Charles A. Hay and Henry E. Jacobs, 3rd edn (Minneapolis: Augsburg, 1875 and 1889), 480.

17. On Spener, see F. Earnest Stoeffler, *The Rise of Evangelical Pietism* (Leiden: Brill, 1965), 238. On Francke, see Peter C. Erb (ed.), *Pietists: Selected Writings* (New York: Paulist, 1983), 156.

18. Bonhoeffer, *Cost of Discipleship*, 47, cf. 312.

19. Bernard McGinn, *The Foundations of Mysticism: Origins to the Fifth Century* (New York: Crossroad, 1991), xvi.

20. *ibid.*, 117-21; 171-80.

21. *The Babylonian Captivity of the Church*, *LW* 36:109.

22. Martin Brecht, *Martin Luther*, vol. 1, *His Road to Reformation 1483-1521*, tr. James L. Schaaf (Philadelphia: Fortress, 1985), 137-44.

23. Arndt, *True Christianity*, Foreword, 24-5.

24. Erb (ed.), *Pietists*, 69.

25. Kittelson, 'Contemporary Spirituality's Challenge to *Sola Gratia*', 378.

26. David S. Yeago, 'The Promise of God and the Desires of our Hearts', *Lutheran Forum* 21 (Pentecost, 1996), 30.

27. 'Spirituality and Spiritual Formation', *Currents in Theology and Mission* 27 (October 2000), 351.

28. Lawrence S. Cunningham and Keith J. Egan, *Christian Spirituality: Themes From The Tradition* (New York: Paulist, 1996), 47-56.

29. *BC*, 12.

30. Lectures on Romans, *LW* 25:478. In this context Luther is commenting on Romans 13:11, 'It is full time now for us to wake from sleep.' He stresses the need for repentance, and just prior to the words quoted above he says, 'To stand still on the way to God is to retrogress.'

31. Arndt, *True Christianity*, Foreword to Book III, 221.

32. John Arndt, *True Christianity*, tr. and ed. Charles F. Schaeffer (Philadelphia: General Council Publication House, 1910), bk. II, chap. 20, 2-4, p. 235.

33. Andreas Aarflot speaks of progress and journey in his thoughtful reflection on 'Patterns of Lutheran Piety', in *The Lutheran Church Past and Present*, ed. Vilmos Vajta (Minneapolis: Augsburg, 1977), 148.

4.   Authority and Sources of Wisdom

1. A definition close to this is used in 'Spirituality and Spiritual Formation', A Position Paper of the Faculty of Lutheran Theological Southern Seminary, *Currents in Theology and Mission* (October 2000), 27:5, 350.

2. The word 'theology' suggests a world view with belief in God. In a secular or non-theistic faith this sort of reflection would better be called philosophy.

3. *BC*, Epitome, 2-8; cf. Solid Declaration 3-13. When some princes thought the document later called the Solid Declaration too lengthy, theologian Jakob Andreae was charged to summarize it and this is called the Epitome. So the *Formula of Concord* consists of two parts.

4. Gunther Gassmann and Scott Hendrix, *Fortress Introduction to the Lutheran Confessions* (Minneapolis: Fortress, 1999), 53.

5. *BC*, article 2, 1-5.

6. *LW*, 35:396.

7. *Joint Declaration on the Doctrine of Justification*, 18. Italics added.

8. 'The Inspiration of Scripture', A Report of the Commission on Theology and Church Relations, The Lutheran Church–Missouri Synod, March 1975.

9. Robert P. Carroll, 'Poststructuralist Approaches: New Historicism and Postmodernism', in *The Cambridge Companion to Biblical Interpretation*, ed. John Barton (Cambridge: Cambridge University, 1998), 61-2.

10. *BC*, Conclusion of Part One, 1.

11. *BC*, Conclusion, 5.

12. Melanchthon develops his argument in greater detail in the *Apology*, article 21.

13. Frank C. Senn, *Christian Liturgy: Catholic and Evangelical* (Minneapolis: Fortress, 1997), 267-85; 329-46; *The Oxford Encyclopedia of the Reformation*, s.v. Liturgy: Protestant Liturgy, by Frank C. Senn.

14. From *Martin Luthers Briefwechsel*, 12:316f. Cited in Senn, *Christian Liturgy: Catholic and Evangelical*, 335.

15. Richard Kieckhefer, 'Major Currents in Late Medieval Devotion', *Christian Spirituality: High Middle Ages and Reformation*, ed. Jill Raitt (New York: Crossroad, 1987), 75-105.

16. *BC, Apology of the Augsburg Confession*, article 21, 10.

17. *Oxford Encyclopedia of the Reformation*, s.v. Catechisms.

18. *ibid.*, s.v. Monasticism and Monasteries.

19. *ibid.*, s.v. Catholic Reformation.

20. *ibid.*, s.v. Church Ordinances and Episcopacy.

5. Attention to the Word

1. *LW*, 31:344-45; Lull, 597-8.

2. For good discussions of law and gospel, see Bernhard Lohse, *Martin Luther's Theology: Its Historical and Systematic Development*, tr. and ed. Roy A. Harrisville (Minneapolis: Fortress, 1999), 267-76, and Gunther Gassmann and Scott Hendrix, *Fortress Introduction to the Lutheran Confessions* (Minneapolis: Fortress, 1999), 55-62.

3. *The Oxford Encyclopedia of the Reformation*, s.v. Bible: Translations of the Bible; Frank C. Senn, *Christian Liturgy: Catholic and Evangelical* (Minneapolis: Fortress, 1997), 305.

4. Marc Lienhard, 'Luther and the Beginnings of the Reformation', in *Christian Spirituality: High Middle Ages and Reformation*, ed. Jill Raitt (New York: Crossroad, 1987), 279.

5. *The Encyclopedia of the Lutheran Church*, s.v. Bible Versions – Norwegian Versions.

6. *The Oxford Dictionary of the Christian Church*, s.v. Preaching.

7. Donald P. Hustad, *Jubilate II: Church Music in Worship and Renewal* (Carol Stream: Hope, 1993), 185.

8. *ibid.*, 179.

9. *The Oxford Companion to Christian Thought*, s.v. Preaching/homiletics.

10. *Concise Encyclopedia of Preaching*, s.v. Berthold of Regensburg, by Arthur G. Holder.

11. *LW*, 31:357; Lull, 609.

12. All the quotations in this paragraph are from *The German Mass and Order of Service, LW*, 53:68-9.

13. Spener, *Pia Desideria*, 87.

14. Senn, *Christian Liturgy: Catholic and Evangelical*, 499-500.

15. Brian Wren, *Praying Twice: The Music and Words of Congregational Song* (Louisville: Westminster John Knox, 2000), 20-1.

16. Hustad, *Jubilate II*, 180-1.
17. Senn, *Christian Liturgy,: Catholic and Evangelical*, 275-9.
18. *Against the Heavenly Prophets*, LW, 40:141.
19. *The German Mass and Order of Service*, LW, 53:61.
20. *ibid.*, 69.
21. Wren, *Praying Twice*, 16-19, 69-70; Andrew Wilson-Dickson, *The Story of Christian Music* (Minneapolis: Fortress, 1996), 66.
22. Wren, *Praying Twice*, 69.
23. Preface to Georg Rhau's *Symphoniae iucundae*, LW, 53:323.
24. Wren, *Praying Twice*, 69
25. *ibid.*, 78. Wren quotes Hustad, *Jubilate II*, 31.
26. Erik Routley, *A Panorama of Christian Hymnody* (Collegeville: Liturgical Press, 1979), 1.
27. Senn, *Christian Liturgy: Catholic and Evangelical*, 346-50.
28. Quoted with commentary in Andrew Wilson-Dickson, *Story of Christian Music*, 89.
29. Senn, *Christian Liturgy: Catholic and Evangelical*, 350-1.
30. *Praying the Word* (Geneva: Lutheran World Federation, 2003), 36-7.
31. *The Lutheran Book of Worship* (1978), *With One Voice* (1995), *Renewing Worship Songbook* (2003), and *This Far by Faith: An African American Resource for Worship* (1999) are published by Augsburg Fortress Press.

6.　Prayer and Devotional Literature

1. *An Exposition of the Lord's Prayer for Simple Laymen*, LW, 42, 20.
2. *A Simple Way to Pray*, LW, 43, 199.
3. *Large Catechism, The Lord's Prayer*, BC, 20.
4. *A Simple Way to Pray*, LW, 43, 200.
5. *ibid.*, 198.
6. *ibid.*, 193.
7. In his otherwise excellent article, the Finnish Luther scholar Simo Peura says Luther used his four-stage meditation on part or all of the Ten Commandments or Creed prior to meditation on the Lord's Prayer. Rather, Luther says he begins by reciting the Commandments and Creed before meditating on the Lord's Prayer, and then if he has time, meditates in detail on the other two. Simo Peura, 'The Essence of Luther's Spirituality', *Seminary Ridge Review* (Winter 2000), 20-1.
8. *A Simple Way to Pray*, LW 43:209.
9. Puera, 'The Essence of Luther's Spirituality', 20.
10. Martin Nicol, *Meditation bei Luther* (Goettingen: Vandenhoeck & Ruprect, 1984).
11. Jean Leclercq, 'Ways of Prayer and Contemplation – Western', in *Christian Spirituality: Origins to the Twelfth Century*, ed. Bernard

McGinn, John Meyendorff, and Jean Leclercq (New York: Crossroad, 1985), 419.

12. Bernard McGinn, *The Foundations of Mysticism: Origins to the Fifth Century* (New York: Crossroad, 1991), xv-xx; *The Growth of Mysticism: Gregory the Great Through the 12th Century* (New York: Crossroad, 1994), x-xii.

13. According to Merton, the beginnings of contemplation retain the sense of distinction between self and God, but when one crosses over into the promised land, that sense of distinction is overcome. Thomas Merton, *New Seeds of Contemplation* (New York: New Directions, 1961), 279-84.

14. Teresa of Avila, *The Life of Teresa of Jesus*, tr. and ed. E. Allison Peers (Garden City: Image, 1960), Chap. 22, pp. 209-13.

15. Gerhard, *Sacred Meditations*, meditation 25, 140.

16. John Arndt, *True Christianity*, ed. Charles F. Schaeffer (Philadelphia: General Council, 1910), bk II, chap. 20, 1-9.

17. *ibid.*, Preface to the Third Book, 1.

18. John Arndt, *True Christianity*, tr. Peter Erb (New York: Paulist, 1979), Forward, 25.

19. Peter C. Erb (ed.), *Pietists: Selected Writings* (New York: Paulist, 1983), 68-9.

20. *ibid.*, 92.

21. Ole Hallesby, *Prayer*, tr. Clarence Carlsen (Minneapolis: Augsburg, 1931), 11.

22. Dietrich Bonhoeffer, *Life Together*, tr. John Doberstein (New York: Harper & Row, 1954), 49.

23. Dietrich Bonhoeffer, *Prayerbook of the Bible*, in *Dietrich Bonhoeffer Works*, tr. James Burtness, vol. 5 (Minneapolis: Fortress, 1996), 155.

24. More detailed listing of devotional writings among Lutherans may be found in *The Encyclopedia of the Lutheran Church*, s.v. Devotional Literature, and in Nicholas Hope, *German and Scandinavian Protestantism*, 1700-1918 (Oxford: Clarendon, 1995).

25. *LW*, 43, 5-10.

26. Hope, *German and Scandinavian Protestantism*, 194-5; 369-70.

27. LW, 42:7, 87, 99.

28. Eric Lund (ed.), *Documents from the History of Lutheranism*, 1517-1750 (Minneapolis: Fortress, 2002), 268.

29. Hope, *German and Scandinavian Protestantism*, 21.

30. *The Encyclopedia of the Lutheran Church*, s.v. Devotional Literature – In America.

31. L. DeAne Lagerquist, *In America the Men Milk the Cows* (Brooklyn: Carlson, 1991), 109.

32. *The Theologia Germanica of Martin Luther*, tr. Bengt Hoffman (New York: Paulist, 1980), 54.

33. Introduction by Peter Erb, *Johann Arndt: True Christianity* (New York: Paulist, 1979), 9-17.

7. Sacraments and Physical Symbols

1. *New Catholic Encyclopedia*, 2nd edn (2003), s.v. Sacramental Theology.
2. *BC, Large Catechism*, 41-2.
3. *ibid.*, 34.
4. *ibid.*, 29.
5. *ibid.*, 65.
6. *ibid.*, 67, 71.
7. BC, *Formula of Concord* – Solid Declaration 7.35.
8. One exception was the proposal of S.S. Schmucker and other supporters of 'American Lutheranism' in the *Definite Synodical Platform* (1855) to rescind the *Augsburg Confession*'s affirmation of real presence. The proposal met with stiff opposition, and the movement faded.
9. Frank C. Senn, *Christian Liturgy: Catholic and Evangelical* (Minneapolis: Fortress, 1997), 315.
10. *Baptism, Eucharist and Ministry* (World Council of Churches: Geneva, 1982), 21.
11. 'The Eucharist as Sacrifice', in *Lutherans and Catholics in Dialogue I-III*, ed. Paul C. Empie and T. Austin Murphy (Minneapolis: Augsburg), 192-7.
12. Senn, *Christian Liturgy: Catholic and Evangelical*, 223-6.
13. *ibid.*, 222-3.
14. *BC*, article 2, 1.
15. Quoted in Senn, *Christian Liturgy: Catholic and Evangelical*, 469.
16. BC, *Large Catechism*, 45-84.
17. Senn, *Christian Liturgy: Catholic and Evangelical*, 501.
18. BC, *Large Catechism*, 32.
19. Senn, *Christian Liturgy: Catholic and Evangelical*, 352.
20. *ibid.*
21. BC, *Large Catechism*, Exhortation to Confession, 13.
22. *The Encylopedia of Religion*, s.v. Roman Catholicism, by Richard McBrien, 437.
23. *Against the Heavenly Prophets in the Matter of Images and Sacraments, LW*, 40:146.
24. 'If I were to speak according to the usage of the Scriptures, I should have only one single sacrament [Christ], but with three sacramental signs', *The Babylonian Captivity of the Church, LW*, 36:18; Lull, 274. In the Vulgate translation of 1 Timothy 3:16, Christ is called 'the sacramentum'. At this point in this treatise, Luther speaks of three sacraments, but later in the same work questions whether repentance and absolution should be so called.
25. 'The Eucharist as Sacrifice', 192.
26. *Historical Dictionary of the Orthodox Church*, s.v. Sacraments.
27. Carl E. Braaten and Robert W. Jenson (eds.), *Christian Dogmatics* (Philadelphia: Fortress, 1984), vol. II, 367-85.